Often refutations of scien

well-meaning lay persons

theological or apologetic training. Ransom Poythress is both an accomplished biologist and a knowledgeable biblical scholar. His commitment is to both the craft of science and the awareness of the reasons people throw up objections to its compatibility with Christian faith. He writes in a sympathetic, non-combative manner which ought to disarm all but the most obdurate skeptic. A must read by anyone concerned with the so-called science-vs-religion controversy.

WILLIAM EDGAR
Professor of Apologetics, Westminster Theological Seminary,
Philadelphia, Pennsylvania

Despite all the efforts of secular scientism, the 'God hypothesis' refuses to go away. Ransom Poythress' book explains, compellingly, why this is so. He directly addresses the questions people have, and the unspoken assumptions behind them, presenting clear, robust, and well-argued answers. This is a book to read yourself, and to give to your sceptical friends.

KIRSTEN BIRKETT
Former lecturer in ethics and philosophy, Oak Hill Theological
College, London
Author of *Unnatural Enemies: An Introduction to Science and
Christianity*

Has Science Made God Unnecessary? addresses one of the most frequent questions I faced as a believer in Jesus when I was a college and graduate student in Physics, and I think it continues to be a challenge to all Christians today, especially the younger generation who are making their way through a secular academy and society. Poythress' simple and careful style of showing the weak philosophical foundations of naturalism and scientism is spectacular – I haven't seen a more accessible and gentle presentation of this critical material anywhere else.

Starting with philosophical questions first may make some people uneasy and question the book's relevance, but Poythress is sensitive to this, noting the importance of examining what we believe and why we believe it. All too often we uncritically absorb the naturalism from culture and modern science without realizing that many of science's key assumptions about the world are borrowed capital from Christianity and cannot be sustained apart from theism. Once one sees that naturalism as a philosophy is bankrupt, one can then be open to considering God and the weighty evidence that science can deliver to answer this question. Indeed, once our eyes are made sensitive to it, the heavens do declare the glory of God after all.

Through the use of simple yet powerful analogies, an easygoing pace, and excellent references for those who want to dig deeper, Poythress reaches any interested reader with an answer that affirms Christianity while respecting and encouraging the proper roles of science. This is a great book for any youth group, college class, or seeker to think through.

JOHN A. BLOOM

Professor of Physics & Director of the MA, Science and Religion program, Biola University, La Mirada, California

Author of *The Natural Sciences: A Student's Guide*

THE BIG TEN
Critical Questions Answered

SERIES EDITORS
James N. Anderson and Greg Welty

Has Science Made God Unnecessary?

Ransom Poythress

CHRISTIAN
FOCUS

Copyright © Ransom Poythress 2022

paperback ISBN 978-1-5271-0773-1
ebook ISBN 978-1-5271-0878-3

Published in 2022
by
Christian Focus Publications Ltd,
Geanies House, Fearn, Ross-shire
IV20 1TW, Scotland
www.christianfocus.com

Cover design by Paul Lewis

Printed and bound by
Bell & Bain, Glasgow

CONTENTS

To my wife, who's ever so patiently teaching me how to write with compassion and grace.

Acknowledgements

This book would not have been possible without the kindness, wisdom, and patience of friends and family who so generously contributed of their time and energy to comment on multiple drafts: Vern and Diane, Jay and Carolyn, Lisbeth, James Anderson, and Greg Welty. Many thanks as well to those working behind the scenes at Christian Focus in editing, formatting, and marketing: Helen Jones, Irene Roberts, and Rosanna Burton. Special thanks to my amazing wife who worked hard to watch the boys in order to gift me the time for long runs to think and pray. *Soli Deo Gloria.*

Introduction:
Understanding the Question

There is no reason to suppose that science cannot deal with every aspect of existence. Only the religious – among whom I include not merely the prejudiced but the underinformed – hope there is a dark corner of the physical Universe, or of the universe of experience, that science can never hope to illuminate. But science has never encountered a barrier, and the only grounds for supposing that reductionism will fail are pessimism in the minds of scientists and fear in the minds of the religious.[1] – Peter Atkins (Former Chemistry Fellow at Lincoln College, Oxford)

The findings of science imply that the belief systems of all the world's traditional religions and cultures... are factually mistaken.[2] – Steven Pinker (Psychology Professor, Harvard University)

1   Peter Atkins, *Nature's Imagination: The Frontiers of Scientific Vision*, ed. John Cornwell (Oxford University Press, 1995), p. 125.

2   Stephen Pinker, *Enlightenment Now: The Case for Reason, Science, Humanism, and Progress* (Penguin, 2018), p. 394.

Although most wouldn't state it quite so fervently, the sentiment remains, tickling the back of our brain: given the advances in science, haven't we outgrown the need for the Christian God? Isn't God just a pre-scientific 'placeholder' awaiting the technological and theoretical breakthroughs provided by the scientific revolution to fill in the gaps and render God obsolete?

Stated another way by Dr. Ian Hutchinson, an MIT professor, 'Rather, the self-congratulatory attitude among the enlightened (including me) was that Christianity had been discovered to be irrelevant and outdated. Its commitment to past ideas was its problem, and those ideas had proven to be ineffective. Those of us who had escaped the religious trammels were free thinkers, finding out by our own efforts and intelligence what was really going on, not only in natural science but also across all the academic disciplines.'[3]

In this short volume, I will examine the idea that science has shown that we don't need God. I hope my treatment is deep, thorough and robust, while maintaining clarity, simplicity and accessibility. But, before we begin in earnest, I think it will be helpful to focus our question and clear up some misconceptions.

---

3 Ian Hutchinson, *Can A Scientist Believe in Miracles: An MIT Professor Answers Questions on God and Science* (InterVarsity Press, 2018), p. 5.

DOES SCIENCE PROVE THAT GOD DOESN'T EXIST?

I hope we can quickly agree that the answer here is a clear 'No.' No one has yet devised a way to walk into a lab, perform a set of controlled experiments, and definitively say that God doesn't exist. Albert Einstein confessed: 'To be sure, the doctrine of a personal God interfering with the natural events could never be refuted, in the real sense, by science.'[4] To 'prove' anything sets a very high standard, and it's not typically a word that scientists use. Given my quick dismissal of this question, I should also be quick to address the flip side:

DOES SCIENCE PROVE THAT GOD DOES EXIST?

In the limited sense that I mentioned, above, we can also say that, No, there isn't a particular set of laboratory experiments that definitively prove God's existence either. So, have we arrived at some sort of evidential impasse where we can say nothing about God's existence? Well, no – although neither side may be able to provide a scientific 'proof' in a laboratory sense, we can consider other kinds of scientific evidence and philosophical proofs. I believe we come closer to the core of the issue by asking:

---

4   Albert Einstein, 'Science and Religion,' quoted in *Religion and the Natural Sciences: The Range of Engagement*, ed. James Hutchinson (Wipf & Stock Publishers, 1993), p. 150.

BY PROVIDING AN EXPLANATION FOR EVERYTHING, DOES SCIENCE SHOW THAT WE DON'T NEED GOD?

Even here though, we need more clarification since it is easy to see that science currently does not explain everything. That would've put all scientists out of a job! So, we can more accurately state the question as:

COULD SCIENCE *EVENTUALLY* EXPLAIN EVERYTHING AND THEREFORE MAKE GOD IRRELEVANT AND REDUNDANT? WILL SCIENCE EVENTUALLY HAVE ALL THE ANSWERS AND PUT GOD OUT OF A JOB?

Herein lies an interesting and compelling question. If science *can* explain everything, then God becomes superfluous. As Laplace, the eighteenth-century scholar and polymath, famously put it when asked why he didn't include references to a Creator in his *Celestial Mechanics* treatise, 'I have no need of that hypothesis.'[5] Without a need for God, why speculate and hypothesize an unnecessary entity that exists so far outside of the bounds of science?

But what happens if science cannot explain everything? This is different from simply saying that science does not currently explain it all. What if, by the very nature and definition of science itself, there are some things that *cannot* be explained by science? How do we explain those things? These are the questions I hope to consider as we progress.

---

5   Pierre Simon de Laplace, quoted in *Science and Religion* ed. Paul Kurtz (Prometheus Books, 2003), p. 78.

PERSONAL REQUEST

Before we begin to examine details, I have a personal request. I'd like to ask that you consider the attitude with which you approach the topic. You and I cannot help but bring our preconceived notions, personal history, and foundational beliefs to any discussion. I realize it's perhaps unreasonable to abandon all defenses or come without any trepidation or suspicions. But insofar as it's possible, the more honest and open we can be, the more we stand to gain.

That being the case, I should say a brief word about true beliefs and the pursuit of truth. All too often we say we want to believe true things, but, in actuality, we want truth to accord with our already established beliefs. It's so much easier that way! It can be very challenging to accept a truth that is inconvenient, uncomfortable or offensive. Scientific studies bear this out. We are prone to deliberately avoid information that counters our beliefs and misinterpret that information if we do see it.[6] If you have ever gotten bad news from a doctor's diagnosis, a poor job evaluation, or a failing test score, you know how hard it can be to accept the truth of those things. Ignorance really can be bliss.

---

6 J.A. Frimer *et al.*, 'Liberals and Conservatives Are Similarly Motivated to Avoid Exposure to One Another's Opinions,' *Journal of Experimental Social Psychology* vol. 72 (2017), pp. 1-12; D. Kahan *et al.*, 'Motivated Numeracy and Enlightened Self-Government,' *Behavioural Public Policy* vol. 1, no. 1 (2017), pp. 54-86.

Similarly, any discussion of God is liable to make us uncomfortable for personal reasons, not scientific or logical ones. It might require a massive shift in thinking. Sometimes we may refuse to accept evidence for fear of what it means practically for our lives. We simply don't want it to be true; however, all our wishing and believing never makes a true thing untrue. When I worked in retail for a while, I had a good friend who would talk philosophy with me during breaks. Eventually our discussions got around to God and, after several talks, he admitted that although there might be evidence for God, he didn't like the idea of a God who would have authority over our lives and to whom we would be accountable. Ultimately, he rejected a possibly true thing because it made him personally uncomfortable.

The aforementioned Dr. Hutchinson candidly confessed as he considered Christianity '…my limited understanding of Christianity told me that being a Christian would close off lots of options – choices, freedoms – about how to live my life. That was a major influence causing me to keep my distance, to hold Christianity at arms' length. I did not want a Lord; I wanted to be my own Lord. I did not spend too much time thinking about whether Christianity was actually true, because I already knew that it was personally inconvenient. I did not much want it to be true.'[7]

---

7   Hutchinson, *Can A Scientist Believe in Miracles?*, p. 6. NYU Emeritus Philosophy Professor Thomas Nagel has expressed similar

Let's be honest: talking about God is scary! There is a lot at stake here. It can be terrifying to ask sincere questions where the answers have a deep impact on the fundamental parts of our life. What if we're wrong? Leading up to writing this book, I didn't want to read some of the evidences and counter-arguments presented in the literature because I was afraid it would shake me at the core. In the end, I decided the cost was worth it in order to pursue truth, and I hope you too will decide that the pursuit is worth the potential worldview upheaval.

Therefore, as Christian theologian C.S. Lewis puts it: 'I can only beg you, before you throw the book away, to consider seriously whether your instinctive repugnance to such a conception is really rational, or whether it is only emotional or aesthetic...Are we mistaking for an intrinsic probability what is really a human desire?'[8] In other words, don't use intellectualism as a smokescreen for a deeper issue. Our heads can rationalize so much while our hearts remain veiled.

If you are contemplating the possibility of God, I'm curious: what would it take to believe that God *does* exist?

sentiments: 'I want atheism to be true and am made uneasy by the fact that some of the most intelligent and well-informed people I know are religious believers. It isn't just that I don't believe in God and, naturally, hope that I'm right in my belief. It's that I hope there is no God! I don't want there to be a God; I don't want the universe to be like that.' Thomas Nagel, *The Last Word* (Oxford University Press, 1997), pp. 130-31.

8   C.S. Lewis, *Miracles* (HarperCollins, 1947 restored 1996), p. 40.

Would you refuse to believe in God unless all other possible explanations have been disproven? Famous evolutionary biologist and atheist Richard Dawkins has confessed that he is not sure *any* evidence could convince him of the existence of a supernatural entity. In this case, Dawkins actually has an *a priori* belief in the non-existence of the supernatural that is not based on scientific evidence. Thus, no experiment could show it to him. For those for whom no amount of evidence is sufficient, could we take a moment to consider how many other things in life we hold to this kind of evidential standard? For example, how do we know we're not living in a very complicated simulation (a la *The Truman Show* or *The Matrix*)? It would be impossible to disprove every conceivable scenario. This is partly why it's so hard to counter conspiracy theorists. No matter how much evidence you pile in front of them, people will always find some loophole or roundabout excuse not to believe you.

If you feel like you're willing to seriously and honestly wrestle with the evidence, then this book is for you. The rest of this book has roughly two sections. The first section (Chapters 1–8) examines whether God's existence is necessary for science to function. The second section (Chapter 9–14) discusses positive evidence for God from within science.

1

The Conflict Thesis

There is no harmony between religion and science. When science was a child, religion sought to strangle it in the cradle. Now that science has attained its youth, and superstition is in its dotage, the trembling, palsied wreck says to the athlete: 'Let us be friends.' It reminds me of the bargain the cock wished to make with the horse: 'Let us agree not to step on each other's feet'.[1] – Robert Green Ingersoll (Agnostic and Early American Orator)

In today's world, the media makes quite a bit of noise about the supposed war between science and religion. However, it is striking to note that, if there is a war, it's a largely one-sided war. Most people writing about the existence of this conflict are non-religious. For the Christian, there is no conflict, nor can there be, for God

---

1   Robert Green Ingersoll, *The Works of Robert G. Ingersoll Vol. 8* (Outlook Verlag, 2018), p. 224.

Himself creates, upholds and sustains a world where science is possible and reveals Himself truly in the natural world. Doing science is consistent with belief in God. We'll look in more depth at a positive case for science from Christianity in Chapter 8.

However, we all feel some sort of tension. Religion and science in the public square don't appear to be harmoniously unified. There can be a very real conflict between different *interpretations* of science or between different beliefs that people *bring to* the sciences. We'll examine a few of those different interpretations later. So, why the confusion? What has happened is that some people have equated their particular interpretation of scientific findings with science *itself.* Science as an enterprise, and the human undertaking and interpretation of science need to be separated and evaluated individually. We'll examine this later as well.

Suffice it to say, the history of science is replete with Christians who unashamedly made progress in the sciences *because* of their Christian faith, not in spite of it. Just to name a few scientists who were also professing Christians: Roger Bacon, Gregor Mendel, Blaise Pascal, Gottfried Leibniz, Robert Boyle, Johannes Kepler, Nicolaus Copernicus, Galileo Galilei, Leonhard Euler, Antonie van Leeuwenhoek, Isaac Newton, Michael Faraday, James Clerk Maxwell and Lord Kelvin. It is simply not true to say that there has been no harmony between science and Christianity historically.

Since it is so famous, the 'Galileo Affair' bears mentioning. Many may have heard that the Christian church suppressed the progress of science and tortured Galileo along the way for espousing heliocentrism instead of geocentrism. The topic has been dealt with in depth in several other books already, but the truth is actually more complicated.[2] Galileo himself was a professing Christian! That means the two opposing sides in this narrative shared the same views about the truth of Christianity. Therefore, it seems unreasonable to paint this as a science vs. religion conflict when both sides agreed on the religious aspect.

It's worth noting that throughout history some Christians have been guilty of attempting to suppress science because they don't like some of the implications of certain scientific theories. However, there is plenty of blame to go around. Scientific findings aren't immune to the surrounding geopolitical and cultural pressures from people of all backgrounds and beliefs. Atheistic scientists initially hindered scientific progress by rejecting the Big Bang Theory, not for scientific reasons, but because of the theory's theistic implications.[3] Even today, various scientific studies that aren't 'in vogue' with current cultural trends

---

2   Dava Sobel, *Galileo's Daughter* (Fourth Estate, 1999); Maurice Finocchiaro, *The Essential Galileo* (Hackett Publishing, 2008).

3   https://www.realclearscience.com/blog/2018/05/14/how_bias_against_religion_prevented_scientists_from_accepting_the_big_bang.html

can easily find themselves attacked, minimized or discarded simply because they don't match the prevailing narrative.

Although this perceived tension known as 'the conflict thesis' was widely promulgated during the nineteenth century, most modern historians of science reject the idea. Gary Ferngren, a History Professor at Oregon State puts it this way, 'Although popular images of controversy continue to exemplify the supposed hostility of Christianity to new scientific theories, studies have shown that Christianity has often nurtured and encouraged scientific endeavour, while at other times the two have co-existed without either tension or attempts at harmonization. If Galileo and the Scopes trial come to mind as examples of conflict, they were the exceptions rather than the rule.'[4]

Stated more emphatically by Colin Russell, a History Professor in England: 'The common belief that...the actual relations between religion and science over the last few centuries have been marked by deep and enduring hostility... is not only historically inaccurate but actually a caricature so grotesque that what needs to be explained is how it could possibly have achieved any degree of respectability.'[5]

---

4   Gary Ferngren (ed.), *Science & Religion: A Historical Introduction* (Johns Hopkins University Press, 2002), p. ix.

5   C.A. Russell, 'The Conflict Metaphor and Its Social Origins,' *Science and Christian Belief*, vol. 1 (1989), pp. 3-26.

HISTORICAL TRAJECTORY

What about the modern situation? There were Christians in the sciences who did good work hundreds of years ago, but the majority of scientists today are not theists, and the number seems to be dwindling. A 2009 Pew Forum Poll found 83% of the general public believed in God compared with only 33% of scientists.[6] Isn't that because better understanding of the sciences leads to disbelief in God? The assumption could be: the better educated you are, the more you believe God isn't real.

We should be very careful not to imply causation from correlation. In other words, there are many possible causes for the discrepancy between the number of theists in the general population vs. scientists. We can't simply declare that it has to do with 'progress' and 'education' without examining other possibilities as well. The 33% of scientists identified as theists would undoubtedly be reluctant to admit they were 'uneducated' or not 'keeping up with progress.' Speaking personally as a published scientist with a PhD in Molecular and Cell Biology and Biochemistry who is also a Christian, I find no conflict between my research and my Christianity. In fact, I find that scientific research supports and bolsters my Christianity.

---

6   https://www.pewforum.org/2009/11/05/scientists-and-belief/

So, why is there a gap between the general public and scientists? It's unlikely that we'll ever be able to decisively narrow it down to a single causative factor, but there are several possibilities that may be contributing to varying degrees:

- *Popularity*: Some people invariably self-identify with whatever group happens to be popular (and wealthy and powerful). When Christianity was the religion of choice among rich patrons in the Middle Ages, people would self-declare as Christians just to make life easy. Nowadays, academic and grant-giving institutions tend to be run by more secular belief systems. So, many people accommodate to match what best suits their interests. In other words, there is probably a significant group of people who'll say they believe whatever serves them best personally. Christianity used to be the culturally popular and acceptable worldview in the West but is becoming less so.

- *Group Self-Selection*: For example, if the Royal Society is full of atheists and the only way to join the society is to be nominated and elected by people already in the Society, it shouldn't be surprising if they tend to select like-minded individuals. Now we're not suggesting that scientists query other prospective scientists about their religious beliefs, but there are more subtle, unintentional ways this could happen. For example, there is increasing evidence that higher education in America is becoming less and less diverse ideologically for this reason.[7] For example, 'when President Barack Obama announced on July 8, 2009, that he would nominate renowned geneticist Francis Collins to be the new director of the National Institutes of Health, a number of scientists and pundits publicly questioned whether the nominee's devout religious faith should disqualify him from the position.'[8]

- *Hostile and Unwelcome Environment*: As a high school student and college undergraduate, I remember multiple instances where teachers or professors would discourage, undermine or ridicule Christians. Even as a graduate student I sat in several meetings where I remember speakers, professors or other students making snide or derogatory comments about Christianity. Fortunately, this doesn't happen everywhere (I hope my circumstances were the exception), but it can be enough to dissuade a talented and eager Christian from pursuing a career in the sciences due to the perceived atmosphere of hostility.

- *Fear of Established Religion and the Role of Higher Education*: Most schools do not teach about how religion

---

7 Almost 40% of top-tier liberal arts colleges in the US have zero Republicans on the faculty. Mitchell Langbert, 'Homogenous: The Political Affiliations of Elite Liberal Arts College Faculty,' National Association of Scholars.

8 https://www.pewforum.org/2009/11/05/scientists-and-belief/

and science can mesh due to fear of promulgating religion in schools, so we're left with the default... a kind of anti-religion sentiment. Nathan Lents, a Professor at John Jay talks about his persuasive tactics: 'I don't really talk about the fact that I am interested in, and working on, their beliefs about evolution. I'm always afraid that if I declare my intentions, they'll put up the intellectual walls and that will be it.'[9] Science cannot be taught in a complete philosophical vacuum (where there are no beliefs about anything). 'Either divine intervention is ruled out in advance or it is not...Yet both are clearly assumptions of a religious nature.'[10] If we are only ever taught one view, without examining alternative hypotheses, is it surprising that many people will cling to that one view? It is possible to teach different views on how science and religion can integrate without 'establishing a religion' as prohibited by the Constitution.

- *Academic and Intellectual Elitism*: Scientists get a lot of respect in today's day and age. Much of this is well-deserved. Getting a PhD is hard (in any discipline) and running a successful research program, acquiring grants and getting published requires creativity, perseverance,

9   Nathan Lents, quoted in David Warmflash, 'Teaching evolution to college students with creationist views requires innovative approaches,' *Genetic Literacy Project*, (January 10, 2020).

10 Thomas Nagel, 'Public Education and Intelligent Design,' *Philosophy & Public Affairs* vol. 36, no.2 (2008), p. 198.

methodological rigor and intellectual excellence. However, being a scientist is not the educational pinnacle, and we should be careful not to overstate our position or elevate ourselves beyond what's reasonable. In some respects, high-level science is very myopic. It has become extremely specialized. We used to joke during my graduate years that writing a dissertation meant learning more and more about less and less until you knew everything about nothing. Hundreds of years ago the greatest scientists did their science *in addition to* other pursuits like theology, philosophy or writing. In fact, doing science hundreds of years ago wasn't even called science, it was called natural philosophy. Because of the massive amounts of technical expertise and knowledge necessary to specialize in the sciences today, many scientists are *less* well-rounded educationally now than they were a hundred years ago. Try asking research scientists how many classes they've taken on the philosophy of science. This elitism may create a kind of intellectual blindness and a resistance to considering alternatives outside their field of expertise.

- *Chronological Snobbery*: This is a term C.S. Lewis invented that represents a distinct subclass of intellectual elitism. It perfectly captures the human tendency to think 'we've arrived.' This kind of hubris can be exemplified by Peter Atkins: 'Scientists...are privileged to be at the summit of knowledge, and to see further into truth than any of their contemporaries.'[11] We sit at the top of the heap looking down at all the fallen theories, societal missteps, and failures of history with judgment and disdain and pat ourselves on the back for having risen above it all. However, if the history of science teaches us anything, it should be humility.

For example, geocentrism (the belief the Earth is at the center of the solar system) was once 'well-established' science. Geocentrism matched observable data, contributed to technological advancement, made novel predictions, and was the predominant scientific consensus. So, what happened? How could educated scientists be so confident *and* so wrong? At the time, geocentrism looked so good because the theory that eventually replaced it – heliocentrism – hadn't even been seriously proposed yet! This is sometimes known as the 'unconceived alternative.' 'In the past our best and well-confirmed theories turned out to be **false**, and therefore there's the distinct possibility that our current theories might be too.'[12] It seems like every generation thinks it has reached the pinnacle of knowledge, but then we

---

11 Peter Atkins, 'The Limitless Power of Science,' in John Cornwell, ed., *The Frontiers of Scientific Vision* (Oxford University Press, 1995), p. 123.

12 Mitch Stokes, *How to Be an Atheist* (Crossway, 2016), p. 104.

look back and see how wrong previous generations were. Should we not also demonstrate such humility? What is 'established' science can be, and has been, overturned. It is quite possible that some of the 'best' theories of today may be overturned (or modified) in the future by new theories we haven't thought of yet!

SUMMARY OF MAIN POINTS

- By and large, religion and science have not been historically opposed.
- Many scientists find no conflict between theism and science, only conflicts between how these disciplines are interpreted.
- The decrease in the number of Christians in science is probably influenced by a number of factors unrelated to the truth of theism. Regardless, truth is not established by majority vote.

2

God of the Gaps Arguments

People think that epilepsy is divine simply because they don't have any idea what causes epilepsy. But I believe that someday we will understand what causes epilepsy, and at that moment, we will cease to believe that it's divine. And so it is with everything in the universe. – Hippocrates (Ancient Greek Physician and 'Father of Medicine')

The 'God of the gaps' argument is a fairly intuitive idea with some logical weaknesses. The idea is that theists tend to inappropriately use God as an explanation for gaps in our knowledge. This can stunt scientific inquiry by leading us to believe that no further investigation is necessary. In reality, many of those 'knowledge gaps' end up being filled through additional scientific study.

First, we should acknowledge that, logically speaking, such a conclusion does not follow from the premise. That is, just because science has filled some knowledge gaps does not *necessarily* mean it can or will fill all of them. However, this doesn't do much to diminish the force of the argument. Since we do see knowledge gaps being filled, what's to prevent science from filling *all* of them? In other words, why think that science can't or won't eventually fill all the gaps? Let's examine this in more detail.

Historically, we now know that many things that were once attributed to the supernatural have natural explanations. We no longer think that lightning is a demonstration of Zeus' thunderbolts, that the earth is held on the shoulders of Atlas, that the movement of the sun in the sky has to do with the passing of Helios and his chariot, or that the seasons are caused by Persephone's regular visits to Hades. We understand a lot more about the way the world works now, and this understanding only seems to be improving as the years pass.

Theists have sometimes been too quick to jump to supernatural explanations when it isn't warranted and to state these explanations with too much confidence. Thus it is with no little embarrassment that such ideas have been retracted. C.S. Lewis states the complaint with aplomb: 'It is the invariable practice of these Christians. On any matter whereon science has not yet spoken and on which they cannot be checked, they will tell you some preposterous fairytale. And then, the moment science makes a new advance and shows (as it invariably does) their statement to be untrue, they suddenly turn round and explain that they didn't mean what they said.'[1] However, we should be careful not to overstate the conclusions too quickly. Are such theistic explanatory failures due to the actual non-existence of God, or due to the problematic and limited interpretations of finite humans? When it comes to Christianity, where exactly has science filled in 'gaps'?

Christians rely on the Bible as God's Word. Hasn't the progress of science shown the Bible to be riddled with errors and therefore unreliable? To the ancients, the Bible could have appeared to be true because they didn't have modern scientific knowledge. Don't we know better now? Scientific study has cleared away gaps that were actually just literalist misreadings and misinterpretations of phenomenological language in the Bible. Such misinterpretations do no harm to the evidence for God's existence or the truth of the Bible. We can understand this intuitively.

Let's take for example the modern usage of 'sunrise.' If I type into my internet browser 'What time is sunrise tomorrow,' my computer helpfully informs me that sunrise is at 5:42 a.m. tomorrow. However, we all know that the sun doesn't actually 'rise.' The earth spins on its axis causing us to experience daylight when we face the sun and night as we

---

1   C.S. Lewis, *Miracles* (HarperCollins, 1947 restored 1996), p. 110.

rotate away from the sun. However, from our vantage point, we don't feel like we're moving. If I were to go out at 5:42 a.m. tomorrow and look on the eastern horizon, it would *appear* to me like the sun is actually rising above the hills of the Genesee Valley.

So, when the Bible says in Ecclesiastes 1:5, 'The sun rises, and the sun goes down, and hastens to the place where it rises,' is it wrong?[2] Well, no, because it's describing the situation phenomenologically, accommodating to the human perspective on the sun. To humans on Earth the sun does appear to rise and set. The Bible is still true, even if from a scientific sense and the perspective of the solar system, the sun doesn't technically rise and set. God wrote the Bible for all humans across all times; therefore, he deigned to use accommodating language for our benefit. However, because of this, sometimes we can misinterpret this use of language in the Bible, leading to the kind of 'gaps' that science has filled.[3]

---

2   Bible references such as Ecclesiastes 1:5 refer to the book called Ecclesiastes, to the first chapter of that Bible book, and specifically to the fifth verse of that chapter. Thus 'bookname xx:yy' refers to chapter xx, verse yy of the book by that name. Most versions of the Bible have a table of contents with page numbers to help readers locate each book by name.

3   Because all language is human, any description (including scientific) is going to be accommodated in some sense and prone to difficulties. Questions of purpose, context and meaning add layers to interpretive human discourse.

For example, let's look at some verses that were used to justify geocentrism:

> Where were you when I laid the foundation of the earth?
>> Tell me, if you have understanding.
> Who determined its measurements—surely you know!
>> Or who stretched the line upon it?
> On what were its bases sunk,
>> or who laid its cornerstone (Job 38:4-6).

A modern (or ancient) reader can clearly see the use of phenomenological and metaphorical language to convey a point. Since humans have no experience with building planets, God addresses Job using a metaphor that Job can understand: building houses. The words 'foundation,' 'measurements,' 'stretched the [measuring] line,' 'bases,' and 'cornerstone' are all building terms. Unfortunately, some individuals misinterpreted this to mean that the earth can't be spinning since foundations don't move. This is analogical language. We all know analogies break down at some point. The earth is not constructed in exactly the same way that a human house is constructed. Therefore, not everything that's true about a house is also true about the Earth. Does this all mean the Bible is untrue? Not at all, unless we call people liars every time they use a metaphor.

So, what does all this mean? Just because science has filled in gaps regarding geocentrism and heliocentrism, it hasn't provided evidence against the existence of God or the truth of the Bible. It has simply filled in a *type* of gap due to human error in interpretation.

Furthermore, this gap concept has yet to deal with the distinct difference between primary and secondary causation. God can perform in these knowledge 'gaps' in supernatural *or* natural ways. For example, God could intervene directly in the planetary orbiting patterns of our solar system, or he could institute precise natural (and discoverable) laws of motion and gravitation as secondary causes that the planets obey. In the Bible, God frequently uses natural processes as secondary causes to fulfill His purposes. To cite one example: 'the LORD hurled a great wind [a secondary cause] upon the sea, and there was a mighty tempest on the sea, so that the ship threatened to break up' (Jonah 1:4). Unfortunately, theists have a tendency to assume when we find a gap, that God has acted in some direct, supernatural way, instead of imagining that God may have designed and used natural, secondary causes as He so often does in the Bible.

It is interesting to point out that, given this understanding of God's work in nature through primary and secondary causation, Christians don't see God as God of the gaps, but God of the whole thing. God doesn't just step in where we don't understand; He's equally involved in the parts of nature we don't understand *and* the parts we do. As theologian Abraham Kuyper put it: 'There is not a square inch in the whole domain of our human existence over which Christ, who is Sovereign over *all*, does not cry: "Mine!"'[4]

Finally, we must be careful not to replace one God of the gaps with another 'god.' Christians should be quick to acknowledge how we've been hasty to appeal to direct divine action when it isn't necessary and be exceedingly careful about such claims. But, non-Christians should be equally careful. It is a temptation for all of us to stick placeholder 'gods' into places where our understanding is lacking. 'Scientists rightly resist invoking the supernatural in scientific explanations for fear of committing a god-of-the-gaps fallacy (the fallacy of using God as a stop-gap for ignorance). Yet without some restriction on the use of chance, scientists are in danger of committing a logically equivalent fallacy-one we may call the "chance-of-the-gaps fallacy." Chance, like God, can become a stop-gap for ignorance.'[5]

Today, you'll frequently read in the scientific literature places where individuals stick words such as 'chance,' 'evolution,' or 'natural processes' as causative explanations for things they don't understand. These words are less

---

4   *Abraham Kuyper: A Centennial Reader*, ed. James D. Bratt (Eerdmans, 1998), p. 488, emphasis original.

5   William Dembski, 'The Chance of the Gaps,' *God and Design* ed. Neil Manson (Routledge, 2003), p. 251.

scary than 'God,' and we're more likely to overlook their error because those words feel more concrete. It is easy (if unjustified) to say, 'God did it because I don't see any other way.' Likewise, it's easy to say 'evolution or chance did it because I don't see any other way.'[6] Now, we're not saying that evolution (or God) didn't do something, but we are saying we should be careful about reactionary responses which insert filler words instead of honestly admitting there are things we don't understand.[7]

In one sense, all scientific hypotheses are 'gap fillers.' No hypothesis is 100% provable. Absolute certainty removes the usefulness of the scientific method. There is always the potential for falsification with additional information that reduces the 'gap' in knowledge. We must ask, given current knowledge, which potential hypothesis most likely explains how the gap was, is, or will be crossed? Let's not forget about unconceived alternatives as well! Are there places where the gaps in scientific theories are getting wider, more numerous and straining the limits of credulity?

---

6   Some twentieth-century models of the universe were proposed (without any evidence) to be sustained by imagined forces of physics ('gap-fillers') in order to avoid theistic implications of the Big Bang.

7   For a more thorough discussion of the 'God of the Gaps' argument, see Stephen Meyer, *Return of the God Hypothesis: Three Scientific Discoveries That Reveal the Mind Behind the Universe* (HarperOne, 2021), pp. 417-30.

It has been disheartening to see so many people (theists and non-theists alike) speak with so much certainty about science and religion. There are abundant unanswered questions in both fields. There is an over-abundance of unfounded confidence sometimes. Theists who say that we fully understand God and there aren't any difficult questions remaining are too presumptuous. Beware also of scientists who say there is no evidence contradicting evolutionary theory, the facts and data are completely in agreement, and no conundrums exist in biology and chemistry. Odd data points occur in every theory which have yet to be explained or which could lay the foundation for the emergence of new theories.[8] Theists and non-theists should both be more transparent about the challenges and weaknesses in their theories instead of pretending they don't exist. Hiding these issues just makes them appear dishonest. We all, (myself included) need to be more humble about what we don't know.

For the rest of the book we hope to see how, in many areas, science has confirmed our need for God by unmasking naturalistic (Godless) explanations as less probable. Evidence also gives increasing weight to the supposition that the world

---

8   For example, why aren't phylogenetic trees (a diagram showing supposed evolutionary relationships between species) consistent for different proteins? For a more theoretical understanding of this point, Thomas Kuhn's *The Structure of Scientific Revolutions* is a good primer.

truly is as the Bible describes and matches what we might expect from the intelligent, personal Creator made known to us in the Bible. Although many questions remain, God provides a consistent, fulfilling explanation, where scientific explanations *in principle* fall short. To accomplish this, we talk about science itself.

SUMMARY OF MAIN POINTS

- Scientific findings have helped us correct some misreadings of the Bible but have not disproven the Bible.
- God can use secondary causes, such as those described by science to operate much of the natural world.
- All the same, we should be careful not to invoke God as a primary, supernatural causation for every unknown phenomenon.
- We should also be careful not to insert other causes such as 'chance' as naturalistic fillers for unknown phenomena.

3

Behind the Curtain of Science, Part 1: Objectivity and Truth

We must stand ready to acknowledge the fragility of our scientific theorizing. All we are ever able to do in natural science is to select the optimal answer to the questions we manage to formulate within the realm of alternatives specifiable by means of the conceptual machinery of the day. And we have no reason to doubt – nay, we have every reason to believe – that the day will come when this conceptual basis will be abandoned, in the light of yet unrealizable developments, as altogether inadequate.[1] – Nicholas Rescher (Philosophy Professor at University of Pittsburgh)

Everyone has some sense of what science is. It involves theories, experiments, data and results. Every biology class I've taken from middle school through graduate school starts with the scientific method. We could

---

1   Nicholas Rescher, *The Limits of Science* (University of Pittsburgh Press, 1999), pp. 29-30.

start there in our pursuit of truth. Just follow the steps of observation, question, hypothesis, prediction, experiment, data collection, data analysis and conclusion. Surely, we can all agree that this methodology is the least controversial and most objective way to discuss God?

Michael Ruse, a philosopher of biology, tries to encompass this understanding in his characterization: 'Science by definition deals only with the natural, the repeatable, that which is governed by law.'[2] This sounds like a simple, objective starting point. Unfortunately, when we probe a little deeper, we quickly see it's not that easy. First, such a narrow usage actually excludes certain kinds of legitimate scientific work.[3]

Second, the scientific method isn't without its own issues because of the *people* doing it. When Francis Bacon, a professed Christian, presented the steps that are now known as the Scientific Method in *The New Organon*, he required that scientists display 'a willingness to discard all personal biases and a desire to know nature as it is undistorted by

---

2   Michael Ruse, 'Will science ever fail?' *New Scientist*, (8 August 1992), pp. 32-5.

3   As Alistair Donald puts it: 'His definition rules out cosmology and the origin and history of life. You cannot repeat those events, and mainstream cosmology cheerfully admits that the laws of physics do not apply in the first moments after the Big Bang.' https://www.uniontheology.org/resources/life/evangelism/faith-and-science-never-the-twain-shall-meet

theories and presuppositions.'[4] Bacon described four 'idols of the mind' (distorting allegiances) that could sully and impinge on the pursuit of scientific knowledge and which must therefore be abolished. They amount to four different kinds of confirmation bias that could destroy the reputability and impartiality of science.[5]

- 'Idols of the tribe' refers to the human tendency to think that our basic perceptions and impressions are correct.

- 'Idols of the cave' refers to distortions based on an individual's environment, ideology, education and perspective.

- 'Idols of the marketplace' refers to problems arising out of discourse. We use words to communicate and words can be misunderstood or fail to perfectly capture ideas.

- 'Idols of the theater' refers to problems arising from adherence to large-scale systems of philosophy, classification or theories.

---

4   Phil Dowe, *Galileo, Darwin, and Hawking* (William Eerdmans Publishing, 2005), p. 66.

5   'Once a man's understanding has settled on something (either because it is an accepted belief or because it pleases him), it draws everything else also to support and agree with it. And if it encounters a larger number of more powerful countervailing examples, it either fails to notice them, or disregards them, or makes fine distinctions to dismiss and reject them, and all this with much dangerous prejudice, to preserve the authority of its first conceptions.' (Book I, XLVI, p. 43 of Francis Bacon, *The New Organon (Cambridge Texts in the History of Philosophy)*, edited by Lisa Jardine and Michael Silverthorne, (Cambridge University Press, 2000.)

This was Bacon's ideal: a pure and rarified endeavor without the human stain.

However, science cannot be done without people and must therefore be affected by people. As much as we might like science to be completely unbiased and objective, people doing science can never be fully detached from their own work or their own presuppositions. The human stain remains and has reverberating effects on the final product.[6] People are always influenced in some way (mostly unconsciously) by the 'idols of the mind.' We can easily seek out and interpret experiments and data to support our theories because they affirm our beliefs, lend prestige, elevate our pride, entrench our position, and sometimes even help us keep our jobs. If this all still seems a bit implausible, ask several people to describe the same object or event. Notice how the individuals will inevitably describe it differently, bringing to bear their own personhood in what draws their attention and how they verbalize it.

If you hear someone say, 'Science shows,' 'science says,' 'science describes,' or 'science proves,' that should immediately throw up red flags for you.[7] Science doesn't

---

6   The 'peopleness' of science can also be a benefit. Many significant advances in the sciences are results of accidents or human error, e.g., discovery of the antibiotic penicillin.

7   '[They] should really have said that scientists have found good evidence…The word "proof" should strictly only be used when we are dealing with deductive inferences. In this strict sense of the

say anything. It's not active. People doing science say things based on their interpretation, and interpretations can vary.[8]

Thus, in the final tally, 'the field of human knowledge is not populated by "brute" facts as such, but only by humanly appropriated facts, and human appropriation always involves human interpretation of some sort.'[9] In other words, science cannot function without human interpretation, and interpretations can be wrong or misleading.

It may seem that this undermines the scientific endeavor in its entirety. Can we trust anything scientists do or say? There does seem to be a tension between Enlightenment thinking that truth is accessible through science, and postmodern relativistic thinking that there is no universal truth. The postmodernist viewpoint says that everything is affected and influenced by cultural, personal, political, financial, and other internal and external factors. Therefore, truth is unobtainable. Of course, 'There is no truth' is a logically self-refuting statement, so postmodernism fails at the start. I remember many years ago the pompous pride I felt when I managed to get a bewildered middle school

---

word, scientific hypotheses can rarely if ever be proved true by the data.' Samir Okasha, *Philosophy of Science: A Very Short Introduction* (Oxford University Press, 2016), p. 19.

8   John Lennox, *God's Undertaker: Has Science Buried God?* (Lion Hudson, 2009), p. 19.

9   Del Ratzsch, *The Battle of Beginnings* (InterVarsity Press, 1996), p. 129.

classmate of mine to confess that 'the only absolute is that there are absolutely no absolutes.' Unfortunately, although I was making a technically sound point, I think I only managed to convince the individual that I was an arrogant bully.

- Despite the problems with pure postmodernism, it is becoming more obvious that we can't fully extract ourselves from our science. So, in a limited sense, postmodernism does have a point and the question remains: why and to what extent can we trust the findings of scientists? There must be *some* truth in science, but how do we know what's true and what isn't?

- Postmodernism wins *if* truth is internal: self-defined, self-contained and self-determined. Because people are different, they will have different 'truths.' But if truth is external to us, we can have confidence in our pursuit while still acknowledging in humility our failures and shortcomings. We pursue a goal outside of us that all people can see and strive for, however imperfectly.

For a pure postmodernist, the universal findings of science are always wrong since everyone's truth is different. For a pure modernist, science is always right, and the effects of the human factor are minimized. In the modernist view, science can become the arbiter of all truth, instead of just a means to pursue truth. Individuals in this camp are more likely to be dogmatic and defensive. There is a middle ground though: real science leaves everything tentative, including long-standing and well-supported theories. In doing science, we are always looking to upend, overturn, revise, and refute.[10] In addition, for the purposes of this book, quibbling over precise disciplinary boundaries won't actually further our goals. In a recent experiment, 70 independent teams were asked to analyze the same data, but arrived at a 'sizeable variation' of results.[11]

As Oxford Mathematician John Lennox has pointed out, 'Statements by scientists are not necessarily statements of science. Nor, we might add, are such statements necessarily true; although the prestige of science is such that they are often taken to be so.'[12] Put another way by Calvin University Philosophy Professor Emeritus Del Ratzsch, 'Science is done by humans and it cannot escape what is inescapably human. Our science is limited to humanly available concepts, humanly available reasoning, humanly shaped notions of understanding and explanation and humanly structured pictures of what the world must be like. How could it be

---

10 Samir Okasha, *Philosophy of Science: A Very Short Introduction* (Oxford University Press, 2016), p. 15.

11 Botvinik-Nezer, R., Holzmeister, F., Camerer, C.F. *et al.* 'Variability in the analysis of a single neuroimaging dataset by many teams', *Nature* (2020).

12 Tim Morris and Don Petcher, *Science and Grace: God's Reign in the Natural Sciences* (Crossway, 2006), p. 237.

otherwise? Science seems to have a serious and incurable case of the humans.'[13] We shouldn't dogmatically cling to a theory, even if it's comforting or appealing to us personally and metaphysically.

We can use the scientific method as a tool to discover true things, but tools are only as good as the craftsman who wields them. No craftsman can completely remove himself from his work. His identity is indelibly stamped on everything he makes. But he can still make good, useful and beautiful pieces. In science, we identify the inherent biases and underlying beliefs we bring to our scientific practice. We try to remove personal biases, even if it's not entirely possible. Despite these shortcomings, we can still produce good, true and useful results from our work.

Finally, starting with the scientific method for our analysis doesn't help us decide whether the method works. It doesn't tell us 'why' we should trust the scientific method or if it has limitations. However, we might ask, 'Who cares why it works as long as it does work?' This is a practical approach and one that many scientists take. They are happy to explore the wonders and intricacies of their particular field of study without considering the broader question of why science

---

13   The National Academy of Sciences says, 'Truth in science, however, is never final, and what is accepted as a fact today may be modified or even discarded tomorrow.' https://www.nap.edu/read/6024/chapter/2#2

works. They do this with great success as well! So, what's the problem with being practical?

It's true, you can do science (and do it well) without understanding why it works. You can also drive a car without understanding every detail of thermal transfer, piston action, internal combustion, gas laws, and all the other concepts of physics that are involved. However, regardless of how little you understand the principles of a car, those principles are still active and make your car work. You *assume* those principles are operational even if you can't name them all yourself. If something in your engine goes wrong, no matter how well you turn the wheel, press the accelerator, or turn the key in the ignition, the car won't go. Similarly, when examining the underlying question of God's relation to science, simply doing science isn't sufficient. In this case, we need to see if science *itself* makes assumptions about God.

For example, the construction of a car makes assumptions about the type of fuel you're using. You can't test whether burning coal will work to propel a vehicle by shoving it down the gas tank. Cars aren't designed to process coal for energy. Similarly, we need to see if the 'construction' of science makes assumptions about God and affects how people go about testing for God.

Finally, it's worth pointing out that we haven't defined 'science!' This is at least partly because no consistent definition seems to exist that everyone agrees on, even in the sciences.

'After all, science is a heterogeneous activity, encompassing a wide range of disciplines and theories. It may be that they share some fixed set of features which define what it is to be a science, but it may not... If so, a simple criterion for demarcating science from pseudo-science is unlikely to be found.'[14] An intuitive sense of the scientific endeavor will be sufficient for our ensuing considerations. Roughly speaking, science involves the testing of hypotheses about the natural world.

SUMMARY OF MAIN POINTS

* Science is not totally objective.
* The scientific enterprise is subject to human interpretation.
* Scientific theories are human interpretations of data, and even well-supported theories can and have been false.
* Despite this, one of the goals of the scientific endeavor is to discover what is true and knowable about the natural world.

---

14 By some definitions, evolutionary theory doesn't even qualify as science! 'Darwinism is not a testable scientific theory but a metaphysical research programme.' Karl Popper, *Unended Quest* (Fontana, Collins. 1976), p. 151.

4

Behind the Curtain of Science, Part II: Materialist Assumptions

The success of physics and its role in grounding other sciences supports a broadly naturalistic, or physicalist, worldview: that all phenomena have physical explanations and that notions such as elan vital or incorporeal souls have no place in serious thought anymore.[1] – George Musser (Contributing Editor at *Scientific American*)

To examine the scientific method and why it works, we must speak in ways that may be new or difficult for some readers. It can be quite challenging to identify and discuss preconceived beliefs or notions. Implicit assumptions are sometimes the hardest to uncover because we either don't think about them or aren't aware we have them. We almost never examine our underlying beliefs and presumptions. Yet, everything starts with belief. From there,

---

1   George Musser, 'Virtual Reality,' *Scientific American* vol. 321, no. 3 (2019), p. 30.

we can ask if a belief is justified. People may claim to start with reason. In reality though, they start with a belief in reason. As British philosopher Isaiah Berlin expressed it, 'There are no ages of faith followed by ages of reason. These are fictions. Reason is built on faith, it cannot replace it; there are no ages that are not ages of both: the contrast is unreal.'[2]

Scientists start with belief in the scientific method, but why is this belief justified? What are the underlying principles of the method that are assumed for it to work as we believe it does?

In the next few chapters we'll examine two contradictory underlying beliefs and see how they affect our ability to do science and to justify why science works: materialism and theism. Materialism is the belief that the natural world (atoms, molecules, energy, etc.) is all there is or ever was. All materialists are atheists by definition. Richard Dawkins defines it this way:

'An atheist in this sense of philosophical naturalist is somebody who believes there is nothing beyond the natural, physical world, no supernatural creative intelligence lurking behind the observable universe, no soul that outlasts the body and no miracles – except in the sense of natural

2   Isaiah Berlin, *Three Critics of the Enlightenment – Vico, Hamann, Herder* edited by Henry Hardy (Princeton University Press, 2000), p. 283.

phenomena that we don't yet understand. If there is something that appears to lie beyond the natural world as it is now imperfectly understood, we hope eventually to understand it and embrace it within the natural.'[3]

This is perhaps most famously and succinctly stated by Cornell astronomer Carl Sagan: 'The Cosmos is all that is or was or ever will be.'[4] This particular kind of belief falls under different names: materialism, naturalism, scientism, physicalism, secularism, humanism, evolutionism, Darwinism or philosophical naturalism. There are subtle differences among various proponents of each ideology, but they generally share a commitment to a material, and only material, world – no supernatural forces and therefore no God.[5]

So how far can this materialist assumption get us? Is a belief in materialism reasonable and justified?

We must be careful not to get our logical streams crossed. Instead of starting with materialism alone and seeing what it necessarily or possibly entails, many scientists start with materialism *and* a predetermined conclusion, i.e. the

---

3   Richard Dawkins, *The God Delusion* (Houghton Mifflin, 2006, 2008), p. 35.

4   Carl Sagan, *Cosmos* (Random House, 1980), p. 4.

5   Not all atheists are technically materialists, but I believe materialism to be the simplest and most consistent form of atheism. Unfortunately, space does not permit us to delve into some of these other related but distinct ideologies.

workability of science. Then they endeavor to make the two fit. Notre Dame Professor Christian Smith portrays it this way: 'Their conclusions, in other words, were to some extent determined before they began to think and write – so it appears to me that they are reasoning to a strongly preferred conclusion, not a logically entailed conclusion…. It seems to me to fall into the cognitive bias of what cognitive and social scientists call "motivated reasoning," that is searching for evidence that confirms what one already believes and wants to continue believing, rather than rationally and even-handedly seeking information that could confirm or disconfirm a particular belief. And that sets up some of our [materialists] to try to force and finesse arguments that in fact do not succeed.'[6]

If we start with a materialistic belief, then matter, atoms and energy can behave any way they want. There isn't any good reason why they behave the way they do. For example, as far as we know, all atoms everywhere at all times have followed particular patterns of behavior, and they all follow the *same* patterns instead of each atom following its own pattern. We codify these patterns in what we call 'laws.' But why? Is there any reason why all atoms must behave the same way and adhere to these 'laws'? Why do they follow any patterns at all? If natural things are all that exist, then the

---

6   Christian Smith, *Atheist Overreach* (Oxford University Press, 2019), p. 43.

universe is just as likely, or even more likely, to be irrational, chaotic and inscrutable. If everything is 'blind and random,' then there's no reason to expect order, repeatability, laws or rationality. Nature just is, and it could all change tomorrow!

It appears materialism can't account for the assumptions necessary for science to work. That is, science depends on some non-scientific and non-material assumptions (like rationality). These assumptions about science are not inferable directly from materialism. Therefore, belief in materialism does not necessarily justify our ability to do science.

This means that materialism makes an unjustified leap from philosophy to assumptions for science. In fact, if materialism is true, we have good reason *not* to trust the scientific method and more reason to be suspicious of not only the scientific method, but our own reasoning. There is no reason why the world is reasonable and rational. There is no guarantee that all our experience isn't just an illusion. In the final assessment, materialism is unable to provide justification for science. The ensuing conclusion would be that we happen to be here and even though there's no reason that science works, it does work, so we'll just go along with it.

We don't seem to have any other choice. It might all be wrong, but we don't see any other way of doing it. We've just been lucky that the earth, the sun, and the universe seem to have followed predictable patterns up to this point, but there's no real reason why that can't change instantly. If materialism doesn't justify our reasoning and rationality, then it can't justify the scientific method which relies on reasoning and rationality. Therefore, although some claim to be materialists, they do not actually behave as if materialism is true.

Let's look at two examples of this unjustified leap in action by atheist Jerry Coyne: 'We don't have faith in the rational intelligibility of the universe: we *try to find out* if the universe is intelligible, and if it obeys rules.'[7] That's a little like trying to say 'we use circles to try to find out if circles exist.' He's assuming the very thing he's trying to prove. Coyne states elsewhere: 'Reason—the habit of being critical, logical, and of learning from experience—is not an *a priori* assumption but a tool that's been shown to work.'[8] This is another example of vicious circular reasoning, a self-defeating concept. You can't use a tool unless you *a priori* assume that the tool exists, and functions, in the first place. As C.S. Lewis put it, 'If the value of our reasoning is in doubt, you cannot try to establish it by reasoning.'[9] Belief

---

7 https://whyevolutionistrue.wordpress.com/2019/02/23/mathematician-john-lennox-embarrasses-himself-by-trying-to-reconcile-christianity-and-science/

8 Jerry Coyne, 'No Faith in Science,' *Slate* (Nov 14, 2013).

9 C.S. Lewis, *Miracles* (HarperCollins, 1947 restored 1996), p. 33.

in materialism doesn't seem to give us a good foundation to trust our own reasoning.

It's tempting to just throw up our hands and give up on inquiry or attempts to justify the scientific method. It's due to arguments like these that we can understand why so many people are frustrated with philosophy. However, just ignoring the questions doesn't make them go away. There may be answers. Failing to pursue proper inquiry means we open ourselves to knowingly believe incorrect things and makes it nearly impossible to criticize other viewpoints.

Leaving aside for the moment whether materialism can justify our reasoning, if we are able to assume that reasoning works, can science still function as a self-contained, all-encompassing unit? This belief, sometimes called 'scientism' and famously formulated by atheist Bertrand Russell, decrees: 'Whatever knowledge is attainable, must be attained by scientific methods; and what science cannot discover, mankind cannot know.'[10] He essentially states that since nothing exists outside of nature and the universe, in principle, everything must be testable and explainable by nature and the universe.

Unfortunately, scientism is a self-contradicting concept, similar to 'I do not exist.' If scientism is true, then scientism itself must be testable and attainable merely by scientific

---

10   Bertrand Russell, *Religion and Science* (Oxford University Press, 1970), p. 243.

methods. Since there is no conceivable way to scientifically test such a statement, the statement itself must be false.[11] Although this may seem a difficult concept to grasp, it has a direct and critical application to the original question we asked at the start of the book:

Could science eventually explain everything and therefore make God irrelevant and redundant? Will science eventually have all the answers and put God out of a job?

If we answer those questions in the affirmative, we have created a self-contradictory statement very near to scientism: 'Science can explain everything.' But, that assertion itself can't be proven scientifically. It isn't explainable or testable by science; therefore it's self-defeating and cannot be true. Therefore, there are intrinsic, philosophical limits to what science can show and what gaps can be filled. There are gaps in our knowledge which science cannot bridge due to the nature of science itself. It's not about just collecting more information. Science, by definition, cannot be the path to all knowledge. Science relies on assumptions and first principles that science itself cannot prove.[12]

---

11 See J.P. Moreland, *Scientism and Secularism* (Crossway, 2018), pp. 49-53.

12 Gödel's Incompleteness Theorems 'place limitations on human knowledge – they demonstrate mathematically that some truths are outside our knowledge, and must remain so. If applied to science, the implication of Gödel's theorems is clear: we will never be able to know everything about our universe because we are part of it.' Amir

Although many are content to demonstrate the defeat of scientism and move on, there are some very important implications for our question about God if scientism isn't true. If science can't explain everything, then the inverse must be true: there exist true things that are not explainable by science. In other words, there *necessarily* exist truths outside the realm of science. There are philosophical facts which science will never explain. These include the key assumptions made by scientists in order to even have a workable mode of inquiry about the world, such as faith in logic, induction, sense perception, intelligibility of the world, criteria of good explanation, etc.[13] None of these assumptions are provable within science; they are brought *to* science. None of this is a gap science in itself *can* fill. That is not a diminution of science, but rather an honest recognition of what it can or cannot do. This limitation of science can be an uncomfortable way to think.

The conclusion may seem inconsequential, but applied to discussions about God, it has far-reaching implications. It means there may be legitimate ways to talk about God that are *outside* of science since science doesn't contain *all* knowledge. It's one thing to say we're not going to talk about

Aczel, *Why Science Does Not Disprove God* (HarperCollins, 2014), p. 236.

13 See also https://www.metanexus.net/science-and-inescapability-metaphysics/

God because science can't experiment on God. It's entirely different to say that because we can't experiment on God, He can't exist.

SUMMARY OF MAIN POINTS

- Materialism cannot provide reasonable justification for the foundational presuppositions necessary for science.
- Some truths cannot in principle be captured by science. In other words, science rests on assumptions that can't be shown scientifically.

5

Behind the Curtain of Science, Part III: Materialist Limitations

Our willingness to accept scientific claims that are against common sense is the key to an understanding of the real struggle between science and the supernatural. We take the side of science in spite of the patent absurdity of some of its constructs...in spite of the tolerance of the scientific community for unsubstantiated just-so stories, because we have a prior commitment... to materialism. It is not that the methods and institutions of science somehow compel us to accept a material explanation of the phenomenal world but, on the contrary, that we are forced by our a priori adherence to material causes to create an apparatus of investigation and a set of concepts that produce material explanations, no matter how counter-intuitive, no matter how mystifying to the uninitiated.[1] – Richard Lewontin
(Harvard Evolutionary Biologist)

---

1   Richard Lewontin, 'Billions and Billions of Demons,' *New York Times Book Review* (January 9, 1997), p. 31.

Although the focus of this book is on science and what science has to say about God, God Himself is not limited by science. In other words, since we know at least some truths exist outside of science's capacity to fully encapsulate or explain them, God could exist outside of the narrow purview of science. Put another way, science can't show that God can't exist since science cannot explain itself. God could be the explanation for science's existence. We have not shown that it must be God, only that it conceivably could be.

Perhaps a picture will help. Imagine using a visible-light telescope called 'science' to examine the sky at night. Using this telescope allows you to see space through the 'lens' of science. The telescope is excellent at detecting previously hidden objects in space and magnifying for studying things we could formerly just barely detect by eye. Many stars and planets that were hidden or invisible before are now revealed. Many fantastic discoveries follow with the hope and promise of more in the future as we refine our telescope. In the midst of all the excitement, it would be a mistake to proclaim that the telescope reveals all things or that everything is detectable by visible-light telescopes.[2]

---

2   Edward Feser uses the analogy of a metal detector in his review of *The Atheist's Guide to Reality.* https://www.firstthings.com/article/2011/11/scientia-ad-absurdum

Unfortunately, this is largely what has happened within scientific discussions about God. All too often, scientists have taken a true thing within science and unjustifiably overextended it. We are too quick to hold up the 'telescope' of science and show all the great and marvelous things we can see – all the truths we have discovered, and then say that *only* what we see with the science telescope is true and real. Just because telescopes have had greater success in finding planets and stars than any other method, doesn't mean that planets and stars are all that exist. Saying that 'science discovers truths about physical causes' (things revealed by the telescope are true) is not equivalent to 'all truths are truths about physical causes' (the telescope reveals all true things). It would be an unverifiable belief to say *only* things accessible to science are true. This doesn't negate the value of science to discover truth. The things seen by science are still true, but the science 'telescope' doesn't show us all things. If the program of natural science is set up at the beginning to focus only on material causes, then it will find only material causes. A telescope set up only to detect visible light will detect only visible light. You don't prove that there are no other kinds of electromagnetic radiation by reporting that you did not detect any.

This is also one of the reasons why methodological naturalism won't work for science. Methodological naturalism represents the idea that science should just focus on natural explanations for natural phenomena, regardless of God's existence/non-existence. It asks us to pretend, for the sake of science, that God is never involved in the world in discernible ways.

However, if God exists, which can't be ruled out scientifically, then there's no logical reason He can't be involved in the world in discernible ways. If He is involved in the world in a discernible way, adhering to methodological naturalism in science would *necessarily* lead you to falsehoods. At this point, we could keep employing methodological naturalism to do science, but we'd have to acknowledge that science is no longer a pursuit of truth. It's the difference between looking at a section of space through a telescope and saying it *could* be totally empty vs. it *must* be empty (and devoid of any other kind of energy or particles). If you insist it must be empty, as methodological naturalism and materialism demand, you will *definitely* be wrong at some points.[3]

It may be helpful to sum up the argument so far by returning to our telescope analogy:[4]

---

3   For more on this see Vern Poythress, *Redeeming Science* (Crossway, 2006), p. 270-271.

4   Because this is an analogy, not an airtight equivalency, if pressed in every detail, the analogy will fail at points.

1. We can successfully use visible-light telescopes to study things in space and this success seems to be increasing as we build on what we've learned.

2. All the things we study are visible through the telescope.

3. Therefore, visible things are the only things (only what is visible exists).

4. Because visible things are the only things, and we can study visible things with telescopes, therefore our telescopes work.

5. So, we start by assuming everything is visible for any discussion.

In this analogy, it's pretty hard to talk about molecules and atoms, let alone x-rays and ultraviolet light, with a 'telescope' person since the person doesn't have a category for other wavelengths outside the visible-light spectrum.[5] Yet, we sometimes see similar lines of reasoning for exclusive materialism in science:

1. We can successfully use science to study things and this success seems to be increasing as we build on what we've learned. [This is intuitive and experiential].

---

5   Difficulties in this kind of conversation are explored in a fascinating book: Edwin Abbott, *Flatland: A Romance of Many Dimensions* (Warbler Classics, 1884, republished 2019). I should also note, this book is meant to be an allegory.

2. All the things science studies are material, physically caused things.
3. Therefore, material, physical things are all that there is. [This doesn't logically follow from point 2].
4. Because the material is all there is, and science works with the material, therefore science works.
5. So, we start by assuming materialism for any discussion.

Naturally, it's difficult to discuss the existence of non-material things with a materialist, since their starting assumption for any conversation is that non-material things don't exist. When we start with materialism as an *a priori* assumption, it effectively closes large areas of conversation as inadmissible. Scientific evidence can become the only kind of permissible evidence. X-rays and gamma rays must become visible colors in order to be considered. It becomes difficult to talk about radio waves if you have to take away its 'radio waveness' and convert it into something it's not. Similarly, it becomes almost impossible to talk about God if you have to take away His 'godness' in order to converse. However, science doesn't have a monopoly on the truth. Thus, if we allow that truth *does* exist outside of the boundaries of science, then we must allow that God, if He exists, may not conform to a materialist understanding. We need to freely think about God apart from the confines of a materialist belief.

Let's look at two very common objections about God that demonstrate this point about materialistic belief in science and its effects: the questions of God's complexity and 'Who made God.'

Richard Dawkins lays out the argument:

> I challenged the theologians to answer the point that a God capable of designing a universe, or anything else, would have to be complex and statistically improbable…Scientific arguments, such as those I was accustomed to deploying in my own field, were inappropriate since theologians had always maintained that God lay outside science…The theologians… were defining themselves into an epistemological Safe Zone where rational argument could not reach them because they had declared by fiat that it could not. Who was I to say that rational argument was the only admissible kind of argument? There are other ways of knowing besides the scientific, and it is one of these other ways of knowing that must be deployed to know God….God,…cannot be, whatever else he might be, simple….God may not have a brain made of neurons, or a CPU made of silicon, but if he has the powers attributed to him he must have something far more elaborately and non-randomly constructed than the largest brain or the largest computer we know.[6]

You'll notice here that he uses complexity and simplicity in materialist ways as measurable quantities in the natural

---

6   Richard Dawkins, *The God Delusion* (Houghton Mifflin, 2006, 2008), pp. 183-5.

world. Then, his materialist beliefs force him to try to squeeze God into the materialist categories of complexity and simplicity, as if the rules that apply to our natural world must also apply to God. For example, 'blue' must fit into our 'red' lens or it doesn't exist.

What if God doesn't fit a specific materialist definition of 'complexity' since He's immaterial?[7] The materialistic assumptions which Dawkins brings to the table disallow any other kind of discussion. You'll also notice how he subtly and unjustifiably replaces 'scientific arguments' with 'rational argument,' thus implying that any argument that isn't scientific is irrational. Even at the end, he's still trying to define God within materialistic categories: God must be 'constructed' with something akin to a material brain or computer.[8] These materialist assumptions are unjustifiably limiting. Scientific evidence of the sort Dawkins enjoys is one *kind* of evidence, but not the only kind of evidence.

Let's look at one final example of how materialist beliefs can handicap our pursuit of truth. Theologian J.I. Packer states the Christian position: 'The answer to the child's question, "who made God?", is simply that God did not

7   This point is developed further in Alvin Plantinga, *Where the Conflict Really Lies* (Oxford University Press, 2011), p. 29.

8   It is interesting to note here as well that despite Dawkins' proclamations of 'scientific argument,' he's actually making a non-scientific argument. Complexity and simplicity are philosophical concepts, not strictly scientific.

need to be made, for He was always there. He exists forever; and He is always the same.'[9] This is a sufficiently explanatory answer unless you *a priori* assume materialism to be true (like Dawkins does). Since most materialists assume that nothing is truly eternal and everything has a material explanation, therefore God must have a material explanation as well. However, starting with materialism creates restrictions that may not apply to God. You can't apply materialistic boundaries to a God who exists outside of them.[10] God's existence would falsify materialism.

Instead of asking 'Who made God,' we should ask 'Why does God *need* to be made?' Material things come from somewhere (and need explanation), but what if God doesn't need to come from somewhere? Why do we expect God, who is immaterial, to behave like something that's material? Why would God need to be made in the same way a universe is made since God is not material like a universe?

Let's go back to our analogy to help us understand this. Many things fit the category of 'detectable by visible-light telescopes,' but not necessarily all things. For example,

---

9   J.I. Packer, *Knowing God* (InterVarsity Press, 1973), p. 69.

10   Incidentally, this is why experiments on the efficacy of prayers can never disprove their effectiveness, because they entail us knowing the mind of God, which we don't, in order to know if the prayers 'worked.' We can, however, know something about God's thoughts, purposes, plans and works because he has revealed himself in the Bible.

ultraviolet light wouldn't be detectable by a visible-light telescope, yet ultraviolet light exists. Similarly, God doesn't fit into the category of 'being made' that applies to what science studies. That doesn't mean God doesn't exist. In fact, if a god existed who could be contained and described using purely materialistic methods, he wouldn't be a true god at all, just a very powerful superhero or villain. Therefore, assuming God does exist, He apparently exists outside the bounds of materialistic science and therefore won't be limited to materialistic explanations.

Summary of Main Points

- Starting with materialist assumptions can limit our pursuit of truth.
- If God exists, we would not and should not expect Him to be containable by or subject to purely scientific methods.

6

Behind the Curtain of Science, Part IV: What's Actually Necessary for Science

In order for science to work, scientists must assume that the universe they are investigating is playing fair, that it is not capable of conscious deceit, that it does not play favorites, that miracles do not happen, and that there is no arcane or spiritual knowledge open only to a few. Only by making the assumption of materialist monism will the scientist be able to trust the universe, to assume that although its workings are blind and random it is for this very reason that they can be depended upon, and that what is learned in science can, to some degree, be depended upon to reflect reality.[1] – American Humanist Association

In reference to the quote above, must we make those assumptions to accomplish meaningful science or will science work fine without some of them? What truths do we actually *need* for science to work and what kind of

---

1   https://americanhumanist.org/what-is-humanism/war-science-religion/

worldview can justifiably give us those truths? Let's examine a few attempts to distill the basic assumptions necessary for science:

The University of Berkeley has an 'Understanding Science' website that's endorsed by the American Institute of Biological Sciences and National Association of Biology Teachers. They list several assumptions which are 'important and are not controversial in science today...:

1. **There are natural causes for things that happen in the world around us...** Science assumes that there is an explanation...that relies on natural causes, just as there is for everything in nature.

2. **Evidence from the natural world can be used to learn about those causes.**

3. **There is consistency in the causes that operate in the natural world.'[2]**

On the surface, these seem unassailable, but you'll notice how the writers have carefully smuggled in unnecessary and perhaps even incorrect assumptions. Yes, there are natural causes for some things, but not necessarily for *all* things. Science will work on natural things, but not everything has to be natural. Thus, science might work on *some* things, but not *everything*.

---

2   https://undsci.berkeley.edu/article/basic_assumptions

Here again, from the National Center for Science Education: science is 'empirically based and necessarily materialist; miracles cannot be allowed.'[3] Unfortunately, it's the light telescope all over again. I don't have to assume only visible light exists (the natural) in order to recognize that visible-light telescopes (science) are pretty good at detecting visible light, that some telescopes are better than others, that telescopes can be improved over time through community effort, etc. In other words, materialism is not a necessary assumption for science. Visible-light telescopes will work fine studying visible light even if wavelengths outside of the visible spectrum exist. So, if materialist assumptions for science are unnecessary, what are the necessary assumptions for science?

Theologian John Frame has proposed a tripartite approach to the foundations of science: you need the world, law and a mind.[4] You need a physical world for investigating, lawful regularities and rational persons who can experience the world and conceive of the laws.

Biology Professor Douglas Axe reiterates this scientific foundation: 'If science is the application of reason and

---

3   NCSE staff, Education and Creationism Don't Mix (Berkeley, CA: National Center for Science Education, 1985), page 3. Quoted in Hugh Ross, *The Creator and the Cosmos* (RTB Press, 2018), p. 183.

4   A similar formulation was put forward by Oxford mathematician Sir Roger Penrose. See https://theconversation.com/arguments-why-god-very-probably-exists-75451

observation to discover objective truths about the physical world, then doing science requires accepting just a few things—none of them controversial. First, we must accept that objective truths exist [law], as we all naturally do. Then we must accept that some of these truths pertain to the physical world [world] and that some of those that do can be discovered through human observation and reasoning [mind]. Since we all engage in this discovery process from an early age, we all naturally accept these propositions. There is nothing more.'[5] You'll notice no materialistic assumptions are necessary.[6]

At this point, we've moved away from the idea that materialism is the only way to approach science. Given this understanding of scientific foundations, other worldviews, like theism, could provide the necessary essential foundational structure for successful science. Before we

---

5   Douglas Axe, *Undeniable* (HarperOne, 2016), pp. 48-9.

6   Additionally, we could find some assumptions underlying human observation and reasoning: 'Every science presupposes faith in self, in our self-consciousness; presupposes faith in the accurate working of our senses; presupposes faith in the correctness of the laws of thought; presupposes faith in something universal hidden behind the special phenomena; presupposes faith in life; and especially presupposes faith in the principles, from which we proceed; which signifies that all these indispensable axioms, needed in a productive scientific investigation, do not come to us by proof, but are established in our judgment by our inner conception and given with our self-consciousness.' Abraham Kuyper, *Lectures on Calvinism* (Eerdmans Publishing, 1931), pp. 131-2.

consider that, where does a starting belief in materialism lead us? Can materialism give sufficient justification and explanation for the mind, laws or the world? In other words, if materialism is true, would we expect any of those three necessary components to exist? Let's look at each in turn.

The mind has proven to be a particularly tricky and intractable problem for materialists. This is because materialism has no clear way of connecting the brain and the mind and no easy way of explaining consciousness. By materialist thinking – our minds, our reasoning, and our brain power –– are just an interpretation of our sensory input. But how do we know that a particular interpretation is correct or true? The only way to confirm is by testing with our senses, but that's what is under suspicion and needs testing in the first place.[7] We don't have good reason to believe that our reasoning is sound or true. The argument becomes a lesson in circular reasoning.

Several different avenues are available at this point. To solve the problem, some, like atheist Daniel Dennett, deny that consciousness exists. But that ends up destroying the foundational assumptions for science. Most materialists are left *believing* they will eventually have an explanation for

---

7   For example, when you look at a tree, how do you know that what you think you see is in fact what's really there? Your eyes (or other senses) could be mistaken. The 'mental picture' you have may not correspond to reality according to materialism.

mind and consciousness, but it's also likely that they won't. Some choose to abandon materialism: NYU Philosophy Professor Thomas Nagel wrote that if we 'still want to pursue a unified world picture, I believe we will have to leave materialism behind. Conscious subjects and their mental lives are inescapable components of reality not describable by the physical sciences.'[8] Theists vindicate trust in mind and reasoning by grounding consciousness and rationality transcendentally. If an immaterial God has created the mind, we can trust that it works. Unfortunately, we can't thoroughly examine the topic of the mind in part since so little is known presently.[9]

Even if materialism can't reasonably explain the mind, do we *need* God? What we've done to this point is show that science needs 'something' that must be imported from outside of science but does that need to be God? We'll examine materialistic claims to explain where the world came from in Chapters 11–14. Let's turn our attention next to the second part of science: the laws necessary for science.

---

8   Thomas Nagel, *Mind and Cosmos* (Oxford University Press, 2012), p. 41.

9   For more on the theistic foundations of human knowledge and reason, see Stephen Meyer, *Return of the God Hypothesis: Three Scientific Discoveries That Reveal the Mind Behind the Universe* (HarperOne, 2021), pp. 439-46.

Summary of Main Points

- Materialism is not a necessary assumption for science.
- In order for science to work, we need a physical world to examine lawful regularities and rational individuals.
- Materialism has no scientific explanation for the mind of rational individuals.

7

Behind the Curtain of Science, Part V: Scientific Laws

The orderliness of nature—the set of so-called natural laws—is not an assumption but an observation. It is logically possible that the speed of light could vary from place to place, and while we'd have to adjust our theories to account for that, or dispense with certain theories altogether, it wouldn't be a disaster. Other natural laws, such as the relative masses of neutrons and protons, probably can't be violated in our universe. We wouldn't be here to observe them if they were—our bodies depend on regularities of chemistry and physics. We take nature as we find it, and sometimes it behaves predictably.[1] – Jerry Coyne (Atheist and University of Chicago Emeritus Professor)

All science proceeds on the assumption that nature is ordered in a rational and intelligible way. You couldn't be a scientist if you thought the universe was a meaningless jumble of odds and ends haphazardly juxtaposed. When

---

1   Jerry Coyne, 'No Faith in Science,' *Slate* (Nov 14, 2013).

*physicists probe to a deeper level of subatomic structure,
or astronomers extend the reach of their instruments,
they expect to encounter additional elegant mathematical
order.[2]* – Paul Davies (Arizona State University Physics
Professor)

Both of these quotes reflect a critical observation, if
perhaps one we typically take for granted. If laws
didn't exist, we wouldn't be here to observe them,
and science wouldn't be possible. We detect and describe
laws through observation, but we must assume they are out
there to detect in the first place. However, the real question
goes unanswered: why are there laws? Why do regularities
exist, *and* why can those regularities be described and
encapsulated by math in rational ways? A host of renowned
atheist and agnostic scientists and mathematicians have
noted this same conundrum:

- '...the fact that there are rules at all to be checked is
  a kind of miracle; that it is possible to find a rule, like
  the inverse-square law of gravitation, is some sort of
  miracle. It is not understood at all, but it leads to the
  possibility of prediction – that means it tells you what
  you would expect to happen in an experiment you have

---

2   Paul Davies, 'Taking Science on Faith,' *The New York Times*,
     (November 24, 2007).

not yet done.'[3] – Nobel Prize-winning Physicist Richard Feynman.

- 'The most incomprehensible thing about the universe is that it is comprehensible.'[4] – Albert Einstein

- 'It's a huge philosophical question: Why does nature speak the language of mathematics?'[5] – President of British Humanist Association Jim Al-Khalili

- 'The first point is that the enormous usefulness of mathematics in the natural sciences is something bordering on the mysterious and that there is no rational explanation for it.'[6] And again: 'The miracle of the appropriateness of the language of mathematics for the formulation of the laws of physics is a wonderful gift which we neither understand nor deserve. We should be grateful for it and hope that it will remain valid in future research and that it will extend, for better or for worse, to our pleasure even though perhaps also to our bafflement, to wide branches of learning.'[7] – Nobel

---

3   Richard Feynman, *The Meaning of It All* (Penguin, 2007), p. 23.

4   Albert Einstein, 'Physics and Reality' (1936), in *Ideas and Opinions*, trans. Sonja Bargmann (Bonanza, 1954), p. 292.

5   https://www.premierchristianity.com/Regulars/Faith-Explored/ The-Atheist-Science-explains-the-universe.-I-don-t-need-God-as-well

6   Eugene P. Wigner, 'The Unreasonable Effectiveness of Mathematics in the Natural Sciences,' *Communications on Pure and Applied Mathematics*, vol. 13 (1960), pp. 1-14.

7   Ibid.

Prize-winning Physicist and Mathematician Eugene Wigner

This is a significant issue recognized by a wide range of esteemed thinkers. Materialism alone doesn't have an answer for why laws exist and why they're discoverable. According to materialism, there's no real explanation for the regularities of nature. There is no expectation that anything would be predictable, understandable, rational or repeatable. Einstein even says, '*a priori* one should expect a chaotic world which cannot be grasped by the mind in any way.'[8] There's no reason, according to materialism, that matter, energy, atoms and anti-gravity follow any laws or patterns. Secondarily, there's no reason why, given those patterns, they are decipherable, understandable and codifiable by humans.

Admittedly, this view of reality could be very confusing. What would a chaotic world, a world without rules even look like? Let's approach this whole idea by grounding it in something people are familiar with: the game of Monopoly. Monopoly has a set of rules that allow players to move in a regular fashion around a board to accomplish a goal.

But what would happen if you placed the game with all its pieces in front of several 3-year-old children *without any rules or instructions*? We'd rapidly discover that without rules,

---

8   Albert Einstein, *Letters to Solovine*, translated by Wade Baskin, with an introduction by Maurice Solovine (Philosophical Library, 1987), pp. 132-3.

the situation approaches chaos. Pieces could move in any direction arbitrarily. No one takes turns. Money and houses are constantly changing value and worth. Tokens that are supposed to be player pieces are now swapped, stolen, or used as currency. Houses and hotels are randomly scattered across the board. Without law and instruction there are innumerable ways of interacting with the parts of the game. It's a mess to make sense of since there's no consistency. This is actually an oversimplified representation of the situation. As I've described it, at least the pieces themselves are following rules. For example, in real chaos there would be nothing keeping the pieces and money on the table. They might float away or even melt, disintegrate, or recombine with one another.

Our universe is a lot like the game of Monopoly. Our universe follows rules and laws. Furthermore, the laws of the universe are such that we can understand them. Even if we discover that Monopoly has rules, they could be written in a language we don't understand. So, where do the laws of the universe come from, and why can we understand them? Given a materialist understanding, we would expect the universe to resemble any of the infinite chaotic possible combinations, not the ordered, law-abiding universe we have. The universe does not logically *have* to be the way it is any more than a set of plastic tokens and a flat board *has* to have rules. However, the universe must necessarily have rules in order for us to do science, the same way a board game has to have rules if it's to be played.

Given the fact that our universe has laws, similar to how Monopoly has rules, what's the most likely explanation? Let's consider, why does Monopoly have rules? In the case of Monopoly, a designer crafted the pieces and board and set the rules. In fact, wherever we find rules or laws in our world, they've been set by some sort of intelligent designer. So, why not a similar explanation for the rules of the universe? We know of nothing else in existence in our universe that has demonstrated an ability to set rules other than intelligent designers.

Even if rules exist, they must be actively enforced. Giving a chaotic group of 3-year-olds all the rules to Monopoly is unlikely to change the outcome unless someone oversees and enforces the rules. Laws are really just descriptions of a force at work. So, what is that force? Where did it come from? A rule itself has no power, but a parent, coming alongside the 3-year- olds can enforce the rules, correcting them and ensuring they are moving the right number of spaces in the game. As far as we know, scientific laws are inviolable for us. We can't make them or break them, and we are powerless to affect them. We aren't making the laws; we're discovering ones that are already there. If scientific law really exists (and most believe it does, since without it, we have no reason to trust anything we do), there must be a lawgiver and enforcer.

As famous eighteenth-century natural theologian William Paley describes it: 'a law presupposes an agent; for it is only the mode, according to which an agent proceeds: it implies a power; for it is the order, according to which that power acts.'[9] So, who set the laws; who enforces them; and why do they have the characteristics they do?

Interestingly enough, the laws themselves can tell us something about the lawgiver. We can infer some things about a designer based on his design. For example, Monopoly was first printed and distributed in the English language which tells us something about the designer's likely first language. The use of property and money for exchange says something about how the designer attributes value. Using the matching of numbered dice rolls with a numbered advancement around the board indicates something about the designer's beliefs about math. We could make all kinds of guesses about the designer based on the colors on the board, the Atlantic City locations, the direction of movement, etc. Notice too, however, that these passive inferences will only get us so far. We would need to actively play the game as well

9   William Paley, *Natural Theology* (Oxford University Press, 2008), p. 9. Even Stephen Hawking has pointed out the materialist conundrum and the need for an enforcing agent: 'What is it that breathes fire into the equations and makes a universe for them to describe?' Stephen Hawking, *A Brief History of Time: From the Big Bang to Black Holes* (Bantam, 1998), p. 174.

as seek out the designer's self-revelation about why certain decisions were made to learn more.[10]

Let's turn to look at the laws of the universe that form the foundation for the scientific enterprise. Scientists believe the properties of scientific laws include:

1. Laws don't change with time.[11]
2. Laws are the same everywhere in the universe.
3. Laws work at all times in the history of the universe.
4. Laws are powerful. In other words, attempting to break a law comes with real world consequences.[12]
5. Laws are rational (understandable).
6. Laws are immaterial. They don't have a physical essence and can't be 'seen.'
7. Laws 'play fair.' Laws themselves are not deliberately deceptive or tricky. There is a 'rightness' and consistency to the way we expect them to behave.[13]

---

10 The modern version of Monopoly was patented by Charles Darrow in 1935 but was heavily based on The Landlord's Game patented in 1904 by Lizzie Magie as an attempt to simply demonstrate some economic theories and principles.

11 If a law does appear to change, it's either not a true law, or it's interacting in some heretofore uncategorized way with another law, or the change is itself dictated by some higher superseding law.

12 Technically, it's not the laws themselves, but the forces that the laws describe.

13 All these properties can sometimes be grouped under the heading 'Uniformity of Nature.'

So, scientists have to believe in law and its qualities in order to be able to trust anything they do in science. So, what might these laws tell us about a lawgiver? Rewriting the list is enlightening:

Properties of Law	Properties of God
Don't change with time	Immutable
Same everywhere	Omnipresent
Work at all times	Eternal
Powerful	Omnipotent
Rational	Rational
Immaterial	Immaterial
Play fair: 'rightness'	Righteous/Just

The very properties of law that scientists must depend on and assume in doing their work are some of the same attributes of the Christian God as revealed in the Bible.[14] Is it just possible that science *needs* God in order to work? That scientific law itself reflects the God of the Bible as Lawgiver?

SUMMARY OF MAIN POINTS

- Given materialism, a universe with lawful regularities is unexpected and unlikely.

- Materialism cannot explain the lawful regularities necessary for science, but the Christian God can.

---

14 For more on this see Chapter 1, Vern Poythress, *Redeeming Science* (Crossway, 2006).

- The particular lawful regularities of our universe share an uncanny resemblance to the properties of God revealed throughout the Old and New Testaments of the Bible.

8

Behind the Curtain of Science, Part VI: Supernatural Assumptions and a Christian Philosophical Foundation for Science

I do not deny that science explains, but I postulate God to explain why science explains. The very success of science in showing us how deeply orderly the natural world is provides strong grounds for believing that there is an even deeper cause of that order.[1] – Richard Swinburne (University of Oxford Emeritus Philosopher)

Most of my friends who don't believe in God would be quick to say we don't *need* God for science. After all, lots of atheists and agnostics have made great discoveries in the sciences and have done so without God. So, even if God were to exist, He's simply irrelevant and unnecessary in the sciences. But is that true?

---

1   Richard Swinburne, *Is There a God?* (Oxford University Press, 1996), p. 68.

If we give a smartphone to someone, he can do a vast array of complicated things with it, all while denying that semiconductors exist or are necessary or relevant to smartphones. This same individual might change his opinion if you were to open up the phone and smash the semi-conductors inside. Until it stops working, it's easy to deny, ignore, or simply take for granted the technology that makes smartphones work. Similarly, it's easy to take for granted God's existence as a necessary condition to make science possible. Unfortunately, God doesn't 'break' in the way smartphones do so that we could see what would happen to science. On the other hand, it's probably quite good that God doesn't break this way since it might annihilate the universe.

If what we're saying is true, we shouldn't be surprised that people who don't believe in God still have no problem engaging quite successfully in scientific undertakings. They may be unwittingly relying on God's existence in order to do their work while verbally denying Him. You can deny God and do science in the same way you can deny aerodynamics and still successfully fly on a plane.

Philosopher Greg L. Bahnsen's work on the theory of knowledge and particularly self-deception 'has helped to show how people manage such paradoxical stances. They believe a certain proposition and also believe (as a second-order belief) that they do not believe it. They have hidden from their consciousness what their actions continue to reveal to others. <u>In their actions they tacitly rely on truths about the world, while verbally</u> and consciously they do not believe that <u>they do</u>.'[2]

This might help explain why it is so difficult to use science to prove the existence of God.[3] <u>Science presupposes God.</u> The very existence of science is a kind of proof or evidence of God. For example, I can't use my own heart in a test to see if my heart is what's keeping me alive, because I would 'cease to function' if it is indeed my heart that's keeping me alive and I decided to stop it for the test. Similarly, we can't use science as some grand, objective arbitrator to test if God exists, because science would cease to function if God didn't exist.[4]

In that case, wouldn't God be obvious? But maybe He is: in the sense that breathing is obvious. We don't consciously think about it, yet we rely on it to do everything. It's only

---

2   Vern Poythress, *Redeeming Science* (Crossway Books, 2006), p. 13.

3   Although we cannot run an airtight, deductive scientific proof experiment for God's existence, science can provide supporting evidence for the existence of God. We will examine some of this evidence in later chapters.

4   'We cannot prove the existence of beams underneath a floor if by proof we mean that they must be ascertainable in the way that we can see the chairs and tables of the room. But the very idea of a floor as the support of tables and chairs requires the idea of beams that are underneath. But there would be no floor if no beams were underneath.' Cornelius Van Til, *Christian Apologetics*, ed. William Edgar (P&R Publishing, 1976, 2003), p. 133.

when we stop to think about it that we become aware of it. We could deny that we breathe, but the very act of denying it necessitates the ability to breathe to even say the words thus undermining the argument. Theologian and philosopher James Anderson describes it this way: 'Even though God cannot be directly perceived like the ordinary things within the universe, it turns out that we cannot make sense of the ordinary things we do perceive – and the universe as a whole – unless God exists. In short, only a worldview centered on a transcendent, perfect, personal Creator can make rational sense of the very things we take for granted all the time.'[5]

Individuals following along up until now might be willing to acknowledge that God could be involved in science. But, can we build a thoroughly robust and justifiable Christian philosophy of science? What would it look like for science if the Christian God *did* exist? What things would naturally and obviously flow from this conception of God?

---

5   James N. Anderson, *Why Should I Believe Christianity?* (Christian Focus, 2016), pp. 96-7. Put another way by theologian C.S. Lewis, 'We may ignore, but we can nowhere evade, the presence of God. The world is crowded with Him. He walks everywhere *incognito.'* C.S. Lewis, *Letters to Malcolm: Chiefly on Prayer* (Harcourt Brace & World, 1964), p. 75.

CHRISTIANITY PROVIDES FOUNDATION AND JUSTIFICATION FOR SCIENCE

As it turns out, when you start with the Christian God, all the necessary pieces for science we discussed earlier fall into place.

1. World – God has created a physical world.

    a. 'In the beginning, God created the heavens and the earth' (Gen. 1:1).

    b. 'For by him all things were created, in heaven and on earth, visible and invisible, whether thrones or dominions or rulers or authorities – all things were created through him and for him. And he is before all things, and in him all things hold together' (Col. 1:16-17).

2. Mind – God has created beings capable of reasoned understanding of the world.

    a. 'Then God said, "Let us make man in our image, after our likeness. And let them have dominion over the fish of the sea and over the birds of the heavens and over the livestock and overall the earth and over every creeping thing that creeps on the earth"' (Gen. 1:26).

3. Law – God has created regularities that we can uncover and describe.

b. 'While the earth remains, seedtime and harvest, cold and heat, summer and winter, day and night, shall not cease' (Gen. 8:22).[6]

Science works because God underlies, upholds, sustains and creates. God Himself is stable. He promises we're not living in an illusion. He created our rational minds to correspond to a fully existing world that He supports with laws revealing His own divine nature. 'For his invisible attributes, namely, his eternal power and divine nature, have been clearly perceived, ever since the creation of the world, in the things that have been made' (Rom. 1:20, see also Ps. 19:1-4a).[7]

So, science works under this conception of God; but with God as Creator, we are also motivated to *do* science. God is under no compunction to make things a certain way. He creates freely. Therefore, we can't simply deduce the way things *must* be based on first principles about God. We must go out and experiment and find out how they're *actually* created. This helps us learn more about God and His limitless genius as well as more about ourselves.[8] Christianity

---

6   For more, see Edgar Zilsel, 'The Genesis of the Concept of Physical Law,' *Philosophical Review* vol. 51, no. 3 (1942), pp. 245-9.

7   Because of this, Christians can't be 'science-deniers.' They may however take issue with certain human *interpretations* of science.

8   For more, see Vern Poythress, *Redeeming Science* (Crossway Books, 2006), 76. See also, Stephen Meyer, *Return of the God Hypothesis: Three Scientific Discoveries That Reveal the Mind Behind the Universe'* (HarperOne, 2021), pp. 24, 251-4.

also fosters respect for nature and a call to honesty and integrity in our work which are essential for fruitful science. Therefore, science connects us vertically to God in worship, horizontally to each other in love, and downwards to the earth and the rest of creation in care and cultivation.

When we start with belief in God, all knowledge, understanding, and practice logically and necessarily flow from what God reveals about Himself and about us through creation and revelation. We see perfect harmony between God's special written revelation in the Bible and the ways He's revealed Himself in nature. This inspires both confidence and humility. We can confidently pursue science because we know that truth exists and that God reveals it to us in nature. But, we also need humility because we are imperfect and finite. We don't know and can't know everything.

We can derive another important conclusion from this view of God. It means there is no war between science and religion. The Bible and nature are not in conflict. Sometimes our *interpretation* of the Bible and our *interpretation* of nature through science can be in conflict, but we know that the conflict is just an apparent conflict: a product of *our* shortcomings and misinterpretations.[9] Since God is the author of all truth, both in nature and in Christianity, science and religion should perfectly complement and harmonize

---

9   Remember from Chapter 2 how certain Bible verses were
      misinterpreted to support geocentrism.

with one another. As I've stated elsewhere, 'the truth we seek from the Bible and from the study of science is the same: truth that derives from God....The Bible and nature cannot be in conflict because God cannot be in conflict with himself.'[10]

Christians start with God and His revealed word in Scripture. If this is true, then it provides a foundation for our reasoning and therefore our science. Our reasoning images God in the special way He created humans. Without God, we'd have to create a foundation somewhere else. Many try to start with human reason or matter, but as we've already talked about, those things have difficulty justifying their own existence, as they need to. They can't claim to be self-contained and self-existent the way God is.

Two science professors at Covenant College have beautifully elaborated on this: 'human knowledge is radically contingent on God and His purposes, as is every other aspect of the created world. God, being who He is, is under no *a priori* obligation to provide humans with his thoughts or to provide humans with certain knowledge of the facts in some abstract formal sense...God Himself is ultimately the maker of scientific knowledge. Human minds are brought into being by Him and held by Him in an appropriate relation to the world according to His purposes. Human knowledge

---

10 Ransom Poythress, *Richard Dawkins* (P&R Publishing, 2018), p. 50.

is made as we submit to the order He has constructed in the universe and as we engage in God-given order-as-task activities…True human knowledge gained about the world through careful scientific investigation is rooted in God's revealing faithfulness as He enables faithful human responses to His revelation.'[11]

Because of this, the more we align with God, the more His existence is revealed. Eventually you can't help but see Him everywhere. You can't ignore Him, and you don't want to. Then you start seeing Him in new, delightful, and unexpected ways. It's similar to a hidden picture drawing.[12] In one of these paintings you might see a landscape scene where the artist has cleverly hidden a human face in the contours of the hills, in the way the bushes are located, and in the road that winds through it all. Once you've seen the face you can't 'unsee' it. The more you study the painting, the more you see the artist's cleverness in directing every aspect of the painting to the face. By the end, you're amazed that there was ever a time you *didn't* see the face. It seems so obvious and so integral to the substance of the painting.

So it is with God. When you start with belief in God, He reveals Himself in exciting ways. For example, we've already

---

11   Tim Morris and Don Petcher, *Science and Grace* (Crossway, 2006), p. 221.

12   https://publicdomainreview.org/collection/the-art-of-hidden-faces-anthropomorphic-landscapes

discussed how God provides a necessary and sufficient explanation for the existence and prevalence of laws. But because He is a personal, loving God, we can also understand now why those laws have some additional properties. For example, mathematical laws are beautiful, and their proportionality is exquisite: simple motion is described by numerical proportions, general motion by calculus, forces by differential equations, and 4-dimensionality by Maxwell's equations.[13]

God's revelation of beauty, harmony and simplicity wonderfully explains why we find objective proportionality subjectively pleasing. Mathematicians have long noted how simple proportions in art are the ones humans are subjectively drawn to. Apart from God, there doesn't seem to be any particular reason this needs to be the case. To use another, more concrete example: musical chords that humans find subjectively pleasing to the ear match objective proportionalities and ratios. God's genius at work! An octave, C to C, is a 1:2 frequency change; a major 5th is 2:3; a major 4th is 3:4; a major 3rd is 4:5.

These 'matches,' these harmonies between properties of God and the way the world is created, are everywhere, and

---

13 Being beautiful doesn't mean being easily apparent, as evidenced by my frequent stumbling and poor grades in college physics and math classes.

we continue to discover and elaborate on them.[14] We are able to see God's power in creation (Ps. 29:3-4, Ps. 68:34-35), glory (Ps. 19:1-4), wisdom (Ps. 104:24, Jer. 10:11-12), love (Ps. 36:6b-7a), justice (Rom. 8:20-22), and faithfulness (Gen. 8:22).

One longtime science teacher describes it eloquently: 'The created universe is nothing less than the personal expression of the Creator, God, to the creature, man. It is not an imperfect and unreal symbol and it is certainly not a machine, nor is it a random jumble called chaos. Rather, putting it simply and succinctly, the world is a word. The unique message of the Bible then is not only that God the Creator is personal, a self-conscious God (Exodus 3:14) who thinks (Psalm 139:17), who feels (Lamentations 3:32), and who wills (Daniel 4:35), but it sets forth quite plainly that His handiwork in its grand entirety is both a revelation and a means of revelation of Himself and His will.'[15]

---

14 'With every new important advance the researcher here sees his expectations surpassed, in that those basic laws are more and more simplified under the pressure of experience. With astonishment he sees apparent chaos resolved into sublime order that is to be attributed not to the rule of the individual mind, but to the constitution of the world of experience; this is what Leibniz so happily characterized as "pre-established harmony."' Albert Einstein, *Ideas and Opinions* (Bonanza Books, 1954), pp. 224-7.

15 Robert Ream, *Science Teaching* (P&R Publishing, 1972), pp. 33-4.

CHRISTIANITY PROVIDES MEANING, HOPE, AND PURPOSE FOR SCIENCE

Within the Christian understanding of God, many difficult or troubling questions vanish: What is our place/purpose/meaning? The world was made for God's glory and for humans to fully glorify and enjoy God forever. This gives unifying purpose to our pursuit of science and a clear definition to our idea of progress.

The Christian understanding of God also addresses another otherwise troubling issue – the question of human insignificance:

As Carl Sagan presents it, 'The Earth is a very small stage in a vast cosmic arena... Our posturings, our imagined self-importance, the delusion that we have some privileged position in the Universe, are challenged by this point of pale light. Our planet is a lonely speck in the great enveloping cosmic dark.'[16] It doesn't exactly paint a rosy, optimistic view.

Astrophysicist Neil deGrasse Tyson puts it another way: 'If your ego starts out, "I am important, I am big, I am special," you're in for some disappointments when you look around at what we've discovered about the universe. No, you're not big. No, you're not. You're small in time and in

---

16   Carl Sagan, *Pale Blue Dot* (Random House, 1994), p. 7.

space. And you have this frail vessel called the human body that's limited on Earth.'[17]

So, how can we explain this conundrum? How can we be both so small, but *feel* so big and important? First of all, size does not necessarily make something insignificant. For example, you don't consider the tiny antibiotic drug that saves your life insignificant. Second, and more importantly, there's a purpose, a reason for our place in the universe.

The Bible clearly states that God made the world human-centric in many ways. He made us in His image and gave us dominion over the rest of creation. He loved us so much, that He sent Christ to die for us so that we don't have to suffer the just consequences of our sin and mistakes (John 3:16). That makes us infinitely special! But what about those who say, 'The spatial and temporal size of the universe gives us reason to be atheists.'[18]

As much as the Bible tells us how we are special in many ways, God reminds us that He is vast beyond our imagination:

> 'For my thoughts are not your thoughts,
>   neither are your ways my ways,' declares the LORD.
> 'For as the heavens are higher than the earth,

---

17 Neil deGrasse Tyson, 'Neil deGrasse Tyson on the New Cosmos', *Moyers & Company,* https://billmoyers.com/episode/neil-degrasse-tyson-on-the-new-cosmos/, (January 10, 2014).

18 Emily Thomas, 'Can Science Prove God Doesn't Exist?' *The Conversation*, (November 2, 2017).

> so are my ways higher than your ways
> and my thoughts than your thoughts' (Isa. 55:8-9).

The impressive size, magnitude, power, longevity, beauty, etc. are all wonderful reminders of a God who is transcendent and infinitely greater than we are. Creation is an amazing mix of human significance *and* insignificance. It's a reminder of how special we are, but also of how great is the God who made us. We sometimes use the theological terms transcendence and immanence to capture this idea.

Every time we start to get too prideful, we only need to look at the universe around us to see how small we are compared to God's plan. Yet every time we start feeling unwanted or unseen, we can again look at the universe to see our uniqueness and how much God must care for us to put us in such a carefully and lovingly designed world. It's a marvelous and confounding concoction of seemingly incompatible ideas, blended to perfection.

> Lift up your eyes on high and see:
>> who created these?
> He who brings out their host by number,
>> calling them all by name;
> by the greatness of his might
>> and because he is strong in power,
>> not one is missing (Isa. 40:26).

> Are not two sparrows sold for a penny? And not one
> of them will fall to the ground apart from your Father.
> But even the hairs of your head are all numbered.
> Fear not, therefore; you are of more value than many
> sparrows (Matt. 10:29-31).

We should point out here that although the Christian view of who God is and how He works and reveals Himself gives a strong foundation for science, it doesn't provide all the answers. Not all of our questions magically disappear and perhaps some new questions surrounding evil, suffering, and other topics come to the forefront.[19] Because we aren't God, we should expect there to be some mystery. Yet, we do have a reasonable and justifiable hope in the God for whom there is no mystery. God reminds us in the Bible that, as special as we are with our unique calling, we are not God and not everything is accessible to us (Deut. 29:29; Job 38:1-42:6).

I love how Christian apologist Cornelius Van Til expresses this: 'As God has self-contained being and all other being has created or derivative being, so also God has self-contained and man has derivative knowledge... Created man is unable to penetrate to the very bottom of this inherently clear revelation. But this does not mean that on this account the revelation of God is not clear, even for him. Created man

---

19 There is not enough space in this book to deal adequately with all
    these questions. Please see other volumes in the Big 10 series for
    more on those inquiries.

may see clearly what is revealed clearly even if he cannot see exhaustively. Man does not need to know exhaustively in order to know truly and certainly.'[20]

Again, we see the dialectical tension of humility and confidence: confidence that God has provided a rational world that we can begin to unravel and understand, and humility that all our reflections will never make us equal to God. We can do science and do it well, but never to completion and the establishment of our hubris.

Let's take a brief look at a specific application of man's limited understanding: the argument against God from 'bad design.' 'The argument usually proceeds as follows: Organism X has a bad, inefficient, or poor design. If God were a good designer, he would have made it differently. Or: Structure Y has no purpose. A good designer would not create something with no purpose or with a suboptimal purpose.'[21]

Notice that this argument first assumes that God would design something the way we would. It assumes that we know God's mind as it were - that we know why something is the way it is or what its purpose is. Human priorities are not necessarily God's priorities. Something may exist

---

20 Cornelius Van Til, *Christian Apologetics*, ed. William Edgar (P&R Publishing, 2003), pp. 32, 77.

21 Ransom Poythress, *Richard Dawkins* (P&R Publishing, 2018), p. 97.

just because it is beautiful, because it can make us laugh, because it is useful ecologically, or adds to human medicine. Not everything has to be efficient from a one-dimensional engineering standpoint. You'll also note that this argument is a 'god of the gaps' (or, more precisely, a purposelessness-of-the-gaps) argument: just because we don't see a good purpose for X now, doesn't mean we'll never discover a purpose.[22] Assuming Organism X has a bad design assumes we know all there is to know about it – there are no other possible explanations for X. This mindset discourages further scientific study and hampers scientific progress. This actually happened in recent history as research into non-coding DNA was held back because it was dismissed as purposeless 'junk DNA.'[23]

SUMMARY OF MAIN POINTS

- The existence of the Christian God provides a complete, coherent and necessary explanation for all three requirements of science: world, mind and law.

- The existence of the Christian God also explains many other things connected to science: the success of non-Christian scientists, motivation for doing science, the

---

22   For example, we now know the appendix is not a useless, vestigial organ as was once surmised, but serves an important role in gut and immune response.

23   For more on this, see Jonathan Wells, *The Myth of Junk DNA* (Discovery Institute Press, 2011).

beauty of science, the humility and confidence to pursue science, meaning, hope and purpose, to name a few.

- The argument from bad design fails since it presupposes a foreknowledge of the mind of God.

9

Miracles

Any belief in miracles is flat contradictory not just to the facts of science but to the spirit of science.[1] – Richard Dawkins (Atheist and Evolutionary Biologist)

Materialism is absolute, for we cannot allow a Divine Foot in the door. To appeal to an omnipotent deity is to allow that at any moment the regularities of nature may be ruptured, that miracles may happen.[2] – Richard Lewontin (Harvard Evolutionary Biologist)

Are miracles possible? This must be preceded by the question, 'Does/Can the supernatural exist?'

If you start with an *a priori* belief that the material world is all that exists, then miracles can't happen. However,

---

1   Richard Dawkins, quoted in David van Biema, 'God vs. Science,' *Time*, (November 5, 2006).

2   Richard Lewontin, 'Billions and Billions of Demons,' *New York Times Book Review* (January 9, 1997), p. 31.

if we start with the possibility that something exists outside nature, then that opens up the possibility of miracles. If God exists, miracles are at least theoretically possible. In what follows, we will only be discussing the possibility of miracles and the implications for science. Time does not allow a full investigation of the extensive existing evidence for miracles.

Part of the issue has to do with the inviolability of the laws of nature. Our description of laws assumes that the universe is causally closed and nothing exists outside of it. However, philosopher Alvin Plantinga points out that 'given this conception of law, if God were to perform a miracle, it wouldn't at all involve contravening a natural law. That is because, obviously, any occasion on which God performs a miracle is an occasion when the universe is not causally closed; and the laws say nothing about what happens when the universe is not causally closed.'[3]

Furthermore, we need to remember the distinction between human understanding of law, and God's understanding of law. Remember, when we state the 'law of gravity,' we're really just stating our discovery of a predictable pattern that we've noticed. 'The law then represents an inductive leap from the particulars to the general pattern.'[4]

---

3   Alvin Plantinga, *Where the Conflict Really Lies* (Oxford University Press, 2011), pp. 82-3.

4   Tim Morris and Don Petcher, *Science and Grace: God's Reign in the Natural Sciences* (Crossway, 2006), p. 144.

Laws, as we formulate them, are just predictive descriptors. There is no humanly endowed power to them. Our laws are approximations and subject to additional fine-tuning. For example, Newton's laws of motion are good estimations, *except at very high velocities.* Our laws are descriptions that may not capture the reality precisely. The world is not obligated to follow our observed approximations of law all the time.

Science professors Morris and Petcher elaborate further: '[H]owever accurate we find Einstein's theory to be as a description of the phenomena, we can never know if we have captured the reality precisely, and in view of the fact that God's purposes are not merely material, it would be surprising if we have.'[5] The further we dig into science, the more we see how we've used models and laws as our best approximations and estimations of some reality that eludes full comprehension. For example, we have mathematical formulas to describe the behavior of a photon as both a wave and particle even though this doesn't make physical sense. Even our model of the atom is just that: a descriptive model – we're not saying this is how the atom *actually* looks in reality.

Therefore, as I've pointed out, 'a miracle is not a violation of the laws of nature; instead, it is a violation of our *expectation*

---

5   Ibid., p. 142.

of the laws of nature. [We don't have] a full and complete grasp of the real laws of nature: the exact words of God… Therefore, when something surprises us, and violates one of *our* "laws," it does not mean that it has violated one of *the* laws – that is – God's spoken word of truth.'[6] Remember, we don't write the laws; we make educated predictions about what they are.

To better grasp this, let's go back to our Monopoly analogy. Imagine you've never played Monopoly before and are observing it being played for the first time. You notice a regular pattern of movement: people roll a die and move a playing piece clockwise the number of spaces equal to the number on the die. You can then formulate a 'law' to that effect: movement proceeds in a clockwise direction as determined by a die roll. All of a sudden though, something strange happens: someone circles the entire board and goes to the 'Jail' spot. The law has been broken. Or has it? Because we are not privy to the rulebook in this scenario, we were unaware of additional rules and circumstances. This 'going to jail' action would be 'miraculous' to a naïve observer, but it fits perfectly within the *real* laws of the game in an orderly, regulated fashion. There are patterns we can figure out, but there are also exceptions. They are all harmoniously governed by the designer through the rulebook. So it is with

---

6   Ransom Poythress, *Richard Dawkins* (P&R Publishing, 2018), pp. 101-2.

the universe. There are patterns that we can figure out and act reliably upon, but we don't have access to God's complete 'rulebook.' We are finite.

Theologian Herman Bavinck states it this way: 'For that reason a miracle is not a violation of natural law and no intervention in the natural order. From God's side it is an act that does not more immediately and directly have God as its cause than any ordinary event, and in the counsel of God and the plan of the world it occupies as much an equally well-ordered and harmonious place as any natural phenomenon.'[7]

> He sends out his command to the earth;
>   his word runs swiftly.
> He gives snow like wool;
>   he scatters frost like ashes.
> He hurls down his crystals of ice like crumbs;
>   who can stand before his cold?
> He sends out his word, and melts them;
>   he makes his wind blow and the waters flow
> (Ps. 147:15-18).

God providentially oversees the ordinary events *as well as* the extraordinary ones. 'The word of God governs the regularities of the seasons, and of night and day. But it also governs the exceptional cases, where God may deviate from

---

7   Herman Bavinck, *In the Beginning: Foundations of Creation Theology* (Baker, 1999), p. 250.

a hitherto observed regularity... The deviation is just as rational as the rationality of his continuing to govern the world in a regular way most of the time. All the works of God harmonize rationally into a unified plan for the entire world, and for the entirety of history....How his entire plan harmonizes is up to him.'[8] Because we're not God, and don't have the ability to comprehend His complete and perfect 'rulebook' for the world, we'll never have an exhaustive understanding of the miraculous (or non-miraculous). We should be equally amazed by and grateful for the regularities as well as the extraordinary and exceptional.

God is involved in upholding, sustaining, concurrently acting upon, governing and accomplishing His purposes in everything: the regular and the irregular. Everything fits harmoniously under God's sovereign control, plan and law – even things that appear to be extraordinary chance events to us (Proverbs 16:33). Miracles frequently break our expectation of the laws at work and the regularities we've observed thus far. As finite creatures, we won't fully understand how they harmoniously fit into God's plan. Perhaps we could add that sometimes supernatural miracles may be 'natural' events that are 'extraordinary demonstrations of God's Lordship – his power, authority, and presence.'[9]

---

8   Vern Poythress, *Redeeming Science* (Crossway Books, 2006), p. 180.

9   John Frame, *Nature's Case for God* (Lexham Press, 2018), p. 121.

No matter how we choose to distinguish natural and supernatural, the end result is the same: the existence of the Christian God and miraculous events in history in no way diminish the usefulness, reliability or motivation to do science. Science is all about investigating regularities. No part of your ability to do science dictates that irregularities are inherently impossible, only uninvestigable by normal means of science. Some things are not regular: the resurrection of Jesus, the end of the world, the beginning of the world. But, God has promised to make many things regular (Genesis 8:22) and therefore investigable by science.

SUMMARY OF MAIN POINTS

- Miracles are a surprising exception to mankind's most educated predictions of the laws of nature but are not a violation of God's laws of nature.
- Miracles do not undermine the scientific endeavor.

10

Evidence: What Does it Look Like?

It is often said, mainly by the 'no-contests', that although there is no positive evidence for the existence of God, nor is there evidence against his existence. So it is best to keep an open mind and be agnostic. At first sight that seems an unassailable position, at least in the weak sense of Pascal's wager. But on second thought it seems a cop-out, because the same could be said of Father Christmas and tooth fairies. There may be fairies at the bottom of the garden. There is no evidence for it, but you can't prove that there aren't any, so shouldn't we be agnostic with respect to fairies?[1] – Richard Dawkins (Atheist and Evolutionary Biologist)

---

1   Richard Dawkins, quoted in 'Editorial: A scientist's case against God,' *The Independent (London)*, (April 20, 1992), p. 17.

TYPES OF EVIDENCE

As we turn to the issue of evidence and evidential support for God, this quote by Dawkins is appropriate to reflect on. We will spend time analyzing the scientific evidence, but what about other kinds of evidence? We've already determined there *are* other kinds of evidence that we can bring to bear in a discussion like this. Some of the evidence for God may not look like the typical, natural, scientific kind since God is not 'natural.'

Dawkins himself admits that there are real questions and avenues of inquiry that we can pursue with respect to God and Jesus Christ that are not available when thinking about fairies. 'Did Jesus have a human father, or was his mother a virgin at the time of his birth?...Did Jesus raise Lazarus from the dead? Did he himself come alive again, three days after being crucified? There is an answer to every such question, whether or not we can discover it in practice, and it is a strictly scientific answer.'[2] We may not be able to perform experiments in a lab to confirm or deny the existence of Jesus, but we can ask whether existing evidence supports or rejects that hypothesis.

There *is* evidence for God where there isn't evidence for fairies. Jesus really existed. People saw Him. He spoke. He did things. These are recorded by eyewitnesses, including

---

2   Richard Dawkins, *The God Delusion* (Houghton Mifflin, 2006), pp. 82-3.

some non-Christians. To some extent we can use scientific tools like archeology to confirm the history of Biblical accounts.[3]

So, what about non-scientific evidence? Must we limit ourselves to scientific evidence and categorically say we won't allow other types? It's a little like saying that we don't believe in the full electromagnetic spectrum (X-rays, gamma rays, etc.) because our eyes have only ever seen the visible light range. But that's all our eyes are capable of seeing. We need to use other things to 'see' X-ray or infrared wavelengths.

Science can only 'see' in a small range. In that range we *can* see evidence for God and this will be the focus of the remainder of the book. But we need to acknowledge that we need other tools to fully 'see' and examine the complete spectrum: metaphysics, philosophy, history and logic. These tools could include:

- Internal testimony of Scripture. The Bible claims or 'self-attests' to be God's word. The Bible backs up that claim by being internally consistent, coherent and without contradiction, bearing all the hallmarks of truth.

- Testimony of the Holy Spirit in our hearts and souls. In other words, God works in our hearts and minds to give us assurance and confidence in the truth of His word.

- Answered prayers.

---

3   See *Why Should I Trust the Bible?*, another volume in the Big Ten Question series, for more on this.

- Historical evidence for miracles.
- Testimony of conscience (right and wrong).
- Historical accounts and artifacts that corroborate Biblical witness.

Some may flinch at the mention of these things. They seem so unsure and unverifiable. It's true, we do have to be careful about these forms of evidence since our understanding is individual, and prone to deception, but we needn't throw them out. As the saying goes, 'abuse does not negate proper use.' Scientific interpretations can be faulty at times, but we don't think the entire scientific enterprise is illegitimate as a result.

EVIDENTIAL STANDARDS

Before we turn to look at specific scientific evidence, it's worthwhile to pause and take stock of where we are personally. The temptation at this point may be to demand an unnecessarily high standard of evidence and thus refuse to believe in God despite rational considerations as Richard Dawkins has done:

> Scientists of a rationalist bent are often challenged to say what might in principle cause them to change their minds and come to regard [materialism] as falsified. What would it take to convince you of something supernatural? I used to pay lip service to the promise that I would become a supernaturalist overnight, the moment somebody showed me some convincing

evidence. But now… I am less sure…. Why would I reject the hypothesis that I was dreaming, or hallucinating, or the victim of a cunning illusion… What could supernatural even mean, other than falling outside our present, temporarily imperfect understanding of science?… We should exercise the same skepticism over all alleged miracles because the alternative to the miracle hypothesis, even though implausible, is nevertheless more plausible than the miracle.[4]

Are these standards too narrow for us to accept any proposed fact? Such demands may be unjustifiably rigorous. For example, it may be impossible to 'prove' with 'sufficient evidence' that someone's wife is not a robot from the future. The man might continue to propose more elaborate and unlikely explanations to avoid the possibility that the woman is actually a flesh and blood human. The husband could invent all kinds of conspiracy theories and science fictions to avoid a conclusion he doesn't want to accept. If we refuse to believe in God until all our questions are answered satisfactorily, and we've explained away the possibilities of illusions, hallucinations, and all conceivable science fictions, we'll never believe in God. But then again, using that same evidential standard, we should never believe in anything.

---

4   Richard Dawkins, *Brief Candle in the Dark: My Life in Science* (Bantam Press, 2015), pp. 202-3.

So, what kind of evidence *would* it take to be persuasive? We should remember that God is not subject to our demands. He's not a puppet on a string that dances at our bidding. It is tempting to continually move the goalposts: 'Yes, that might be true, but what about....' When I was in high school, my whole class took a bus trip down to Washington D.C. for a museum visit. When we arrived, my best friend and I were in a discussion about the existence of God and miracles. It was a particularly overcast day with low cloud cover and my friend demanded: 'If God is real, have a fighter plane fly under the clouds.' I prayed and a few minutes later an F-16 fighter jet screamed past us in full view under the clouds. My friend immediately turned to me and countered: 'That wasn't a real test – have the fighter jet crash into the Washington Monument.'

Now, I didn't expect my friend to fall on his face and worship immediately upon seeing the jet, but it does illustrate a point. Just because there is an easy, natural explanation for the appearance of the jet, doesn't mean it can't *also* be another point in a long string of evidences for God. If God really is sovereign over all circumstances at all times, then that fly-by was part of His plan and was an affirmative answer to prayer.

Although these types of 'non-scientific' evidences are not the focus of this book, science certainly can't dismiss them outright as inadmissible evidences for God. We may have all kinds of mechanical and logistical explanations for plane flight, but no scientific explanation can exclude the possibility that, among other things, the plane's appearance at that moment was as an answer to prayer.

In the end, how does the evidence for God compare with the evidence against God? Which gives us a more satisfactory picture? Which side is grasping at straws, reaching for more and more absurd and far-fetched explanations? Are things getting easier to explain, or harder? Hopefully, we've already seen that Christian belief provides a solid philosophical justification for the scientific endeavor. It can easily explain why science works where other ideologies struggle. So, someone might agree that God could exist, but still ask if belief in God is to be preferred to unbelief (or non-belief)? Is there positive scientific evidence that would lead someone to prefer God over not-God?

SELECTIVE SHARING AND ALTERNATIVE HYPOTHESES

There is a lot of evidence. This will surprise no one, but perhaps what has not been considered is how critical the *presentation* of that evidence is. It is easy for people to adopt a strategy called 'selective sharing.' An article in *Scientific American* describes the problem: 'This approach involves taking real, independent scientific research and curating it, by presenting only the evidence that favors a preferred position....Selective sharing can be shockingly effective at shaping what an audience of nonscientists come to believe about scientific matters of fact. In other words, motivated actors can use seeds of truth to create an impression of uncertainty or even convince people of false claims.'[5]

Theologian Vern Poythress puts it another way: 'One must not, indeed, "ignore the facts." But every [theory] is confronted with anomalies that are difficult to explain. Every [theory] tends to talk about its successes and to concentrate on problems that the method has some hope of solving, rather than on what is most intractable. If one is trying to choose between [theories]… one must avoid being intimidated by people who appeal to "the facts." Such people are most often thinking of those facts that (they think) prove their case. Other facts, less easily explained, are not mentioned.'[6]

To attach this idea to something tangible, think about politics. Just read two different accounts of the same political event, one from a conservative viewpoint, and one from a liberal viewpoint. Notice how different facts are drawn into the discussion and different quotes are used. The quotes and facts may be real, but they've been selected by the author for a purpose.[7]

---

5   Cailin O'Connor and James Owen Weatherall, 'Why We Trust Lies,' *Scientific American* vol 321, no. 3 (2019), p. 61.

6   Vern Poythress, *Science and Hermeneutics* (Academie Books, 1988), pp. 129-30.

7   Selective sharing, straw man arguments, and double standards have become rampant in media today. Much of the polarization in

But that's politics, not science. Even in the sciences though, there's too much data to present simultaneously, so we must be selective about what gets shared. That process of selection will necessarily reveal our own biases. Wikipedia, for example, is supposed to be a neutral and unbiased source of information. Although it's by no means perfect, it's a source that many people turn to for their 'first-take' on issues. However, many pages related to science and religion are controlled and edited by people opposed to religion.

The co-founder of Wikipedia, Larry Sanger himself points out the problems: 'As the originator of and the first person to elaborate Wikipedia's neutrality policy, and as an agnostic who believes intelligent design to be completely wrong, I just have to say that this article [on intelligent design] is appallingly biased. It simply cannot be defended as neutral…I'm not here to argue the point, as I completely despair of persuading Wikipedians of the error of their ways. I'm just officially registering my protest.'[8]

Therefore, you shouldn't be surprised if, in what follows, you encounter lines of argument that are new and unfamiliar.

---

politics (as perhaps in science) may be attributable to this.

8   Larry Sanger (talk) 05:30, 8 December 2017 (UTC) https:// en.wikipedia.org/wiki/Talk:Intelligent_design. See also https:// evolutionnews.org/2017/12/wikipedia-co-founder-calls-wikipedia-entry-on-intelligent-design-appallingly-biased/ For more on Wikipedia bias see https://larrysanger.org/2020/05/wikipedia-is-badly-biased/

Much time, energy, and money has been invested in a purely materialist paradigm for the sciences. It has become entrenched and there's a vested interest in preserving it. This is normal and natural. It's actually quite good for science that scientists defend and resist changes to large-scale theories. Philosopher of science Thomas Kuhn explains why this is important: 'By ensuring that the paradigm will not be too easily surrendered, resistance guarantees that scientists will not be lightly distracted and that the anomalies that lead to paradigm change will penetrate existing knowledge to the core... [Scientists] will devise numerous articulations and *ad hoc* modifications of their theory in order to eliminate any apparent conflict.'[9] Eventually though, if enough deep questions remain unanswered or unsolvable, alternative theories will gain prominence.

This is largely what happened with geocentrism (the belief that the earth is the center of the solar system). Geocentrism was the scientific consensus of the day and scientists fought to suppress and counter the new heliocentric model (with the sun at the center of the solar system). Geocentrism made novel predictions and contributed to technological advancements. Scientists of the day were convinced that the theory was so central to science that it was impossible

---

9   Thomas Kuhn, *The Structure of Scientific Revolutions* 4th Ed. (University of Chicago Press, 2012), pp. 65, 78.

that the theory was false. Of course we now know that geocentrism is completely incorrect.

So, do we have a modern-day equivalent to geocentrism? Is it possible that a Christian view of the world and the sciences presents a better alternative than the current majority belief in purely materialistic explanations? We shouldn't let the scientific consensus blind us to legitimate alternative hypotheses. For example, suppose I wanted to prove to you that Santa Claus exists. So, on Christmas Eve I leave a plate of milk and cookies in front of the chimney. The next morning, the plate is empty. Santa exists! You of course, being a bit more skeptical, would point out that although my makeshift experiment does support my hypothesis, it has failed to eliminate many other legitimate alternative hypotheses that are also supported by the disappearing food. Our parents could have eaten it while we slept, or our pets, a devious sibling, or a rat, or a robber breaking into the house. Any one of these could explain the situation.

Unfortunately, all too often science can function like the Santa example. Scientists will point to a particular experiment as verification for a materialist view, and forget, or fail to see that other theories (like a Creator God) are also supported by the same evidence. Most of the time though, the 'non-God' position is just assumed. This is not good science, and it's a bit disingenuous to pretend that alternative hypotheses don't exist. This is sometimes referred to as the 'problem of theory underdetermination.'[10] There is always more than one hypothesis that matches the current evidence.

So, how do we choose between hypotheses? Why don't we seriously entertain the idea that a robber broke into your house to steal milk and cookies on Christmas Eve? Well, we must determine which of the available hypotheses is best. But, how do we determine what's 'best'? In part, we can compare certain benchmarks like coherence, explanatory power, parsimony, and other kinds of evidence. However, the complete answer is more complex, and it turns out that prior knowledge, dispositions and beliefs come into play in choosing between theories. In other words, we bring our subjective personhood, history and biases to the table. We can't be completely objective in this process.[11] As philosopher James Anderson clarifies, 'My point is *not* that one scientific theory is ultimately as good as any other, or that there can be no rational basis for favoring one theory over its competitors. Rather, the point is that scientists cannot rely *solely* on observational evidence to establish their theories. They have to rely on other criteria to select between alternate theories—and that's exactly what happens in practice, even if the scientists don't realize it. What's

---

10 For more, see Kyle Stanford, 'Underdetermination of Scientific Theory,' ed. Edward N. Zalta, *The Stanford Encyclopedia of Philosophy,* 2017. https://plato.stanford.edu/entries/scientific-underdetermination/

11 See Chapter 3 as a refresher.

more, those other criteria are typically philosophical—even religious—in nature.'[12]

So, the good news is that there is evidence to think about and evaluate, and more keeps coming. This helps to eliminate or at least diminish the likelihood of some hypotheses. The bad news is that no one comes to the evidence with a blank slate, and it's almost impossible to determine how much our preferences and predilections are influencing us. Everyone leans certain ways toward the evidence. The problem isn't so much the amount or quality of the evidence 'out there' but the disposition of our hearts towards the evidence. The really, really bad news is that if as a result you begin to consider Christianity seriously, you will confront a personal challenge. You will find that you have been actively (if perhaps subconsciously) suppressing the evidence of design testifying to God's presence, suppressing your conscience, and suppressing God's presence inside you. Even Dawkins admits it: 'The illusion of purpose is so powerful that biologists themselves use the assumption of good design as a working tool.'[13] This is painfully difficult for us to admit. Accepting the message of Christ means accepting that He is Lord, and that ends up reconfiguring everything.

---

12 James Anderson, 'Can We Trust the Bible Over Evolutionary Science?' *Reformed Faith & Practice*, vol. 1, no. 3 (2016).

13 Richard Dawkins, *River Out of Eden: A Darwinian View of Life* (Basic Books, 1995), p. 98.

Everything. The stars look different. The machinery in the cell is different. Food looks different. Your own mind is different, because it is indwelled by the Holy Spirit. You lose the walls that surround you, built to keep God out, and begin to see the beautiful world that's always been there, just blocked from view by the self-made fortifications.

So, what about this book? How can you trust that I'm presenting a fair picture of the situation and not doing my own selective sharing? I'll be honest: I'm not completely objective. I can't be. I simply can't present every argument for and against my position. This book wouldn't hold it all! No one can be completely objective. In fact, we should be immediately suspicious of anyone who claims to be completely unbiased and objective.

However, in an effort to demonstrate that I'm trying to be as authentic and transparent as possible, I've done something that I think is almost unprecedented. In the Appendix of this book, I've suggested some reading that presents the most popular arguments *against* my position. Obviously, even the selection itself will reveal some of my bias, but I've tried my best. I've avoided technical literature, but if you're interested in that, most of the suggested books will reference those. I wanted to primarily present the most accessible and well-known literature, not necessarily the highest scholarship since much of that is inaccessible to the average reader. I believe many of the arguments I'll be presenting in the coming chapters haven't been adequately answered, if they've been addressed at all. When you finish this book, pursue more reading. Read replies and responses on both sides of the issue. Try to avoid an echo chamber that just bounces back your own view and reinforces a single position. Examine the best that each side has to offer.

With this background established, let's spend the remaining chapters of this book reviewing the scientific evidence. Does the existing evidence fit Christian claims? As our knowledge expands, are we left with more questions for theism or materialism? Given the evidence, which seems to be the 'better' explanation? Let's look and see if nature screams the existence of God. We will examine four areas of scientific investigation to test the explanatory power of theism versus materialism:

1. Origin of the Universe: Big Bang
2. Fine-tuning of the Universe
3. Origin of Life
4. Development of Complex Life

SUMMARY OF MAIN POINTS

- Various types of non-scientific evidence support the claims of Christianity.
- Data and its interpretation are not presented in an ideological/metaphysical vacuum.

- Presentation of evidence is heavily influenced by the presuppositions of the presenter and the way in which the information is curated: what is shown and what is held back.
- Our own beliefs and worldview affect how we interpret evidence that is shown to us, so we should intentionally engage multiple perspectives.

11

Big Bang and Fine-Tuning

If we are to be honest, then we have to accept that science will be able to claim complete success only if it achieves what many might think impossible: accounting for the emergence of everything from absolutely nothing. Not almost nothing, not a subatomic dust-like speck, but absolutely nothing. Nothing at all. Not even empty space… We shall, in a sense, need to model nothing, and to see if its consequences are this world.[1] – Peter Atkins (Former Chemistry Fellow at Lincoln College, Oxford)

Astronomy leads us to a unique event, a universe which was created out of nothing, one with the very delicate balance needed to provide exactly the conditions required to permit life, and one which has an underlying (one might say 'supernatural') plan.[2] – Arno Penzias (Nobel Laureate and Cosmologist)

---

1   Peter Atkins, *Nature's Imagination – The Frontiers of Scientific Vision*, Ed. John Cornwell (Oxford University Press, 1995), pp. 131-2.

2   Arno Penzias, quoted in William Dembski, *Signs of Intelligence* (Brazos Press, 2001), p. 168.

Our universe had a beginning.[3] This simple statement has some significant implications for scientists. When the Big Bang Model of the universe was first proposed, some scientists vehemently resisted it, not for scientific reasons, but for theological ones. When Albert Einstein heard about the Big Bang model, he recoiled: 'No, not that, that suggests too much the creation.'[4] As recently as 1989, the editor of the premiere science journal, *Nature*, declared the model 'thoroughly unacceptable' because of what it might mean about a Creator.[5] After all, Genesis 1:1 says, 'In the beginning, God created the heavens and the earth.'

The founding director of NASA's Goddard Institute for Space Studies commented on these inconsistencies: 'Theologians generally are delighted with the proof that the Universe had a beginning, but astronomers are curiously upset. Their reactions provide an interesting demonstration

---

3   The Borde-Guth-Vilenkin (BGV) Theorem shows that all current cosmological models necessitate some kind of beginning event. 'With the proof now in place, cosmologists can no longer hide behind the possibility of a past-eternal universe. There is no escape; they have to face the problem of a cosmic beginning.' Alexander Vilenkin, *Many Worlds in One: The Search for Other Universes* (Hill and Wang, 2006), p. 176.

4   Albert Einstein, quoted in John Farrell, *The Day Without Yesterday* (Thunders' Mouth Press, 2005), p. 100.

5   John Maddox, 'Down with the Big Bang,' *Nature* vol. 340 (August 10, 1989).

of the response of the scientific mind – supposedly a very objective mind – when evidence uncovered by science itself leads to a conflict with the articles of faith in our profession.'[6]

Attempts to explain away the issue of the origin of the Universe and its decidedly theistic implications have generally crumbled in face of further scientific investigation. The Steady State Universe hypothesis, various Bouncing Universe theories such as the Infinitely Oscillating Universe Model and Thermodynamic Dissipation within Oscillation, and Quantum Cosmology Models have fallen out of favor in light of the evidence.[7] The current popular theory is the Multiverse model which states that we exist in one universe amidst a host of universes (possibly infinite) that are popping into existence. Although an intriguing model that gives rise to all kinds of fantastic science fiction scenarios (see multiverse scenarios and alternate timelines in many comic book series), it is untestable, unverifiable, unobservable

---

6   Robert Jastrow, *God and the Astronomers* (Warner Books, 1980), p. 5.

7   Steven Hawking's quantum cosmology model without an initial singularity is an interesting mathematical model, but has no correspondence to the real universe: 'When one goes back to the real time in which we live, however, there will still appear to be singularities... Only if [we] lived in imaginary time would [we] encounter no singularities... In real time, the universe has a beginning and an end at singularities that form a boundary to space-time and at which the laws of science break down.' Stephen Hawking, *A Brief History of Time: From the Big Bang to Black Holes* (Bantam Books, 1998), p. 136.

and unfalsifiable. Therefore, it doesn't fit within most definitions of 'science.'[8] As one science writer puts it, 'These theories are attractive to some few theoretical physicists and philosophers, but there is absolutely no empirical evidence for them. And, as it seems we can't ever experience these other universes, there will never be any evidence for them.'[9]

Furthermore, it doesn't actually solve the question at hand. The existence of some place where universes are popping into existence has to be explained as well. For example, suppose we've just arrived on Mars for the first time. We disembark and suddenly a line of cars starts coming toward us from over a nearby hill. You exclaim, 'Where did they come from?' to which I calmly reply, 'They were made in the auto factory just over that hill.' In all likelihood, you won't be content with this answer since you'll want to know how an auto factory ended up on Mars. Similarly, you can't satisfactorily explain our universe 'car' by saying it came from a multiverse 'factory.'

The further back you push, the more you demand an answer to the question 'Where did that come from?,' the closer you'll get to the 'something from nothing' answer which is where it must ultimately lead. Yet, we all know,

---

8   The 'multiverse argument is a well-founded philosophical proposal but, as it cannot be tested, it does not belong fully in the scientific fold.' George Ellis, 'Cosmology: The untestable multiverse,' *Nature*, vol. 469 (January 2011).

9   Jim Baggott, 'But is it science?' *Aeon*, (October 7, 2019).

something has never been observed to come from nothing, and there's no reason to think it ever would, despite the proclamations of some.[10] The 'something from nothing idea' is unfortunately all speculative assertion without evidence. In the end, is it possible that people are reduced to fantastical and far-fetched fairy tales because they don't like the idea of teleology (purpose) in our world?[11] Some philosophers have further pointed out that science *in principle* cannot explain the origin of the universe since a universe must already exist for science to work in the first place.[12] Nobel Laureate Steven Weinberg has confessed we have no way of knowing (scientifically) what caused the Big Bang.[13]

---

10 'Since "nothing" is as simple as it gets, we cannot expect it to be very stable. It would likely undergo a spontaneous phase transition to something more complicated, like a universe containing matter. The transition of nothing-to-something is a natural one, not requiring any agent.' Victor Stenger, *God: The Failed Hypothesis* (Prometheus Books, 2007), p. 133.

11 'Some people are uncomfortable with the purposefully created world. To come up with things that contradict purpose, they tend to speculate about things they haven't seen.' Arno Penzias, quoted in Denis Brian, *The Voice of Genius: Conversations with Nobel Scientists and Other Luminaries* (Basic Books, 2000), p. 164.

12 'A scientific explanation cannot be used to explain the very thing (the universe) that must exist before scientific explanation can get off the ground.' J.P. Moreland, *Scientism and Secularism* (Crossway, 2018), p. 139.

13 Amir Aczel, *Why Science Does Not Disprove God* (HarperCollins, 2014), p. 101.

What about laws? Can't they help us here? Stephen Hawking has famously said, 'Because there is a law like gravity, the universe can and will create itself from nothing.'[14] And ASU Physics Professor Paul Davies agreed: 'I have never liked the idea of divine tinkering: for me it is much more inspiring to believe that a set of mathematical laws can be so clever as to bring all these things into being.'[15] Note that just because something is inspiring doesn't make it true.

However, laws have never created anything. They are not generative. Laws don't *do* anything. They're descriptors.[16] You need a force acting behind a law. And at this point, we've just come back to our original question: 'Where did this force or law come from originally?' For example, a Monopoly rulebook can't make the physical board and

---

14 Stephen Hawking and Leonard Mlodinow, *The Grand Design* (Bantam Press, 2010), p. 180.

15 See Clive Cookson, 'Scientists who glimpsed God,' *Financial Times*, (April 29, 1995), p. 50.

16 'They produce no events: they state the pattern to which every event…must conform, just as the rules of arithmetic state the pattern to which all transactions with money must conform – if only you can get hold of any money… For every law, in the last resort says: "If you have A, then you will get B". But first catch your A: the laws won't do it for you.' C.S. Lewis, *Miracles* (HarperCollins, 1947 restored 1996), pp. 93-4. Or, stated differently: 'Physical laws do not generate or describe complex sequences, whether functionally specified or otherwise; they *describe* highly regular, repetitive, and periodic patterns of events.' Stephen Meyer, *Return of the God Hypothesis: Three Scientific Discoveries That Reveal the Mind Behind the Universe*' (HarperOne, 2021), p. 286, also p. 432.

pieces. A rulebook cannot make itself. The rule book needs someone *outside* the game to print the board, write the rules, and enforce them as the game is played. This all fits coherently with the conception of a supernatural God who sits outside time and space and can create time, space, laws, forces and universes. In this case, God doesn't need explanation or beginning, since He's not natural. The rules that apply to the natural world, such as causation, don't apply to Him.

As we can see, science hasn't adequately explained (nor can it) the existence of the universe or the existence of scientific laws. Nothing can't produce something. But there's yet another problem which we haven't addressed to this point. We've talked about laws in *general* and why laws exist at all, but what about these *particular* laws? For example, the cosmological constant is a mathematical term that's part of Einstein's equations of general relativity. The constant has the value 1.1056×10^{-52} m^{-2}. Why is the constant thus? In other words, in a universe with laws, what if the value of the cosmological constant were different?

It's possible that it doesn't make a difference. Maybe we could pick any random value for the cosmological constant and our world would be basically the same. However, scientists have found that this isn't the case. In fact, if the value of the constant were just a tiny bit smaller, the universe would have collapsed before any stars had the chance to form, and life would be impossible. If the constant were just a tiny bit larger, the universe would have expanded too rapidly and galaxies wouldn't have been able to form. No life would have been possible in that scenario either. The cosmological constant seems to be set at the perfect value to allow and sustain life in this universe. It appears to be 'finely-tuned' for life. Yet, scientists can't explain why the constant is so precisely set. There's no particular reason it couldn't have been at any other value apart from a God who planned accordingly.

This is called the fine-tuning argument. And it doesn't just apply to the cosmological constant. Although the precise and perfect value for the cosmological constant is remarkable, the more we study our universe, galaxy and planet, the more we find these amazing 'coincidences.' One atheist observed, 'A common-sense interpretation of the facts suggests that a superintellect has monkeyed with physics, as well as with chemistry and biology, and that there are no blind forces worth speaking about in nature. The numbers one calculates from the facts seem to me so overwhelming as to put this conclusion almost beyond question.'[17] Over time, the evidence for this fine-tuning has grown, not diminished.

Paul Davies admits that 'scientists are slowly waking up to an inconvenient truth – the universe looks suspiciously like

---

17   Fred Hoyle, 'The Universe: Past and Present Reflections,' *Engineering & Science* (November, 1981), pp. 8-12.

a fix. The issue concerns the very laws of nature themselves. For 40 years, physicists and cosmologists have been quietly collecting examples of all too convenient "coincidences" and special features in the underlying laws of the universe that seem to be necessary in order for life, and hence conscious beings, to exist. Change any one of them and the consequences would be lethal.'[18]

According to astrophysicist Hugh Ross, 'The list of design characteristics for our solar system grows longer with every year of new research. What were 2 parameters in 1966 grew to 8 by the end of the 1960s, to 23 by the end of the 1970s, to 30 by the end of the 1980s, to 123 in 2000, to over a thousand today.'[19] The more time passes and the more science uncovers, the less likely it seems the universe is a product of chance.

Even avowed atheists have admitted that our universe is remarkably fine-tuned. Stephen Hawking said, 'It would be very difficult to explain why the universe should have begun in just this way, except as the act of a God who intended to create beings like us.'[20] And Fred Hoyle: 'I do not believe that any scientists who examined the evidence would fail

18 Paul Davies, *The Guardian,* June 25, 2007. https://www. theguardian.com/commentisfree/2007/jun/26/spaceexploration. comment

19 Hugh Ross, *The Creator and the Cosmos* (RTB Press, 2018), p. 218.

20 Stephen Hawking, *A Brief History of Time: From the Big Bang to Black Holes* (Bantam Books, 1998), p. 127.

to draw the inference that the laws of nuclear physics have been deliberately designed.'[21]

It's a bit like walking into an office building for work. You rarely think about how the carefully tuned temperature, humidity, lighting, spacing, ceiling heights, Wi-Fi, paint colors on the wall, etc., make your day more comfortable and productive, unless something goes wrong. So it is with our universe. We haven't fully grasped the degree to which the entirety of the universe seems to be set *just right* for us.

So, it's very finely tuned, but how finely tuned? Could we get this kind of outcome by a roll of the dice? Nobel Laureate 'Roger Penrose has calculated—based on only one of the hundreds of parameters of the physical universe—that the probability of the emergence of a life-giving cosmos was 1 divided by 10, raised to the power 10, and again raised to the power of 123. This is a number as close to zero as anyone has ever imagined. (The probability is much, much smaller than that of winning the Mega Millions jackpot for more days [in a row] than the universe has been in existence.)'[22]

---

21   Fred Hoyle in Mervyn Stockwood (ed.), *Religion and the Scientists: Addresses Delivered in the University Church, Cambridge* (SCM Press, 1959), p. 64. 'To insist otherwise is like insisting that Shakespeare was not written by Shakespeare because it might have been written by a billion monkeys sitting at a billion keyboards typing for a billion years.' Clifford Longley, 'Focusing on Theism,' *London Times* January 21, 1989, p. 10.

22   Amir Aczel, 'Why Science Does Not Disprove God,' *Time*, April 27, 2014. If you were to try to write this number without using

At what point do we start to consider a personal, thoughtful designer God as a possibility? Imagine rolling a die. You need it to come up six; and it does. That's great. What would you attribute that to? Suppose you rolled a 1000-faced die 1000 times, and it still came up six every time. Would you begin having suspicions that the die might not be random? Perhaps there has been some tinkering, some purposeful design involved? The odds are much worse than that. If you rolled a million-sided die every second of your life and it always turned up six, you'd still be far short of the odds of 'rolling' our universe.

Are there alternative explanations that explain the design in our universe without resorting to a designer? The first way to deal with extreme improbability is to find a way to give yourself *a lot* of chances. The multiverse model that we mentioned earlier accomplishes this – you'd have many different universes with many different constants in each, and ours just happens to be the right combination. However, aside from the fact that the multiverse is purely speculative and untestable, it still doesn't solve the problem.

---

exponents, you would need more zeros than there are elementary particles in the universe. For the original calculation, see Roger Penrose, *The Emperor's New Mind* (Penguin Books, 1989), pp. 339-45.

Any mechanism for creating all these universes would have to have some finely tuned rules and laws itself.[23]

The other common way to dismiss fine-tuning uses a concept known as the anthropic principle. The basic idea is that however improbable our universe and our existence may be, it happened and we are here to observe it. 'In other words, the probability of the fine-tuning of the universe given that we are here is far greater than the simple probability of the fine-tuning of the universe…The problem is partly that it uses something in the future to explain something in the past…[Consider a twenty gun firing squad.] The probability of all twenty guns misfiring is extremely low, but given that you are alive the probability of that coincidence is about one. Does this mean that the fact that you are alive explains the misfiring of the rifles? Certainly not in any normal, direct sense. A later event cannot explain earlier events. The misfiring could be explained in terms of somebody's desire that you survive at a later time.'[24] Similarly, given the incredible fine-tuning of our universe, it seems reasonable

---

23 Furthermore, the multiverse model commits what's known as the Inverse Gambler's Fallacy. Just because we live in a highly improbable universe (based on chance) does not necessarily mean that there must be other 'unsuccessful' universes out there.

24 Phil Dowe, *Galileo, Darwin, and Hawking* (William Eerdmans Publishing, 2005), p. 153.

to conclude that someone desired that we live and survive in this world.[25]

So, we can see, science has not explained why the universe is so finely tuned. It has certainly shown, and continues to show, that it *is* finely tuned. But apart from God, it's difficult to discern any rational reason *why*.

SUMMARY OF MAIN POINTS

- Science has confirmed that our universe had a beginning and that it is remarkably fine-tuned for our existence.
- Materialism cannot provide an explanation for the origin of the universe, laws or the particularly fine-tuned constants in our universe.
- The eternal God of Christianity provides a satisfactory explanation for the creation of our universe and its particular laws.

---

25 Just because our existence *depends* on fine-tuning doesn't mean our existence *explains* fine-tuning.

12

Origin of Life

The origin of life field is a failure – we still do not have even a plausible coherent model, let alone a validated scenario, for the emergence of life on Earth.[1] – Eugene Koonin (Evolutionary and Computational Biologist at NCBI)

An honest man, armed with all the knowledge available to us now, could only state that, in some sense, the origin of life appears at the moment to be almost a miracle, so many are the conditions which would have had to have been satisfied to get it going.[2] – Francis Crick (Nobel Prize Winner and co-discoverer of the structure of DNA)

---

1   Eugene Koonin, *The Logic of Chance: The Nature and Origin of Biological Evolution* (FT Press, 2011), p. 391.

2   Francis Crick, *Life Itself, Its Origin and Nature* (Simon & Schuster, 1981), p. 88.

Despite pronouncements to the contrary, scientists today have no better ideas about how life came to be than we did 70 years ago. To understand the issue, it's necessary to review some biology. For life to exist, we need information. That information has to be readable and transmittable, much like an instruction manual. In this case, instead of building a house or a piece of IKEA furniture, we're building a living cell. Instruction manuals are composed of paragraphs made up of words, consisting of letters that are arranged in meaningful ways. Cells don't have English words, but they do have DNA, RNA, and proteins. Like words, DNA, RNA, and proteins are made from smaller subunits (like letters in our words) that can be combined together in meaningful ways. DNA and RNA have four 'letters' called nucleotides, and proteins have 20 'letters' called amino acids. Without letters, you can't make words, and without words and sentences, you can't have instruction manuals. Without instruction manuals you can't get the final product, in this case, cell life.

But what about all those sensational headlines? 'A Leading Mystery of Life's Origins is Seemingly Solved,'[3] 'Researchers May Have Solved "Missing Link" Mystery in Origin of Life,'[4]

---

3   Nicholas Wade, 'A Leading Mystery of Life's Origins is Seemingly Solved,' *New York Times*, May 14, p. 2009.

4   Jesse Emspak, 'Researchers May Have Solved "Missing Link" Mystery in Origin of Life,' *NBC News*, June 8, 2015.

or 'Found: the origin of life.'[5] Hasn't this issue been solved? Although there's no small debate about it, some scientists think they've found that, under the right conditions, with careful preparation, with elaborately designed systems, and using theoretical early-earth atmosphere, random reactions can generate some of the 'letters' of life from RNA or proteins. Once you have letters, given enough time, the instruction manual is inevitable, right?

There are at least two main difficulties here. The first is that there is an incredible amount of sophistication and intelligent design necessary to get these experiments to run.[6] This actually demonstrates how unimaginably difficult it would be to make these origin of life scenarios without intelligence. One origin of life researcher 'noted that it resembled a golfer, having played an 18-hole course, claiming that he had shown that the golf ball could have, through some combination of wind, rain, heating, cooling, dehydration, and ultraviolet irradiation played itself around the course without the golfer's presence.'[7] This particular

---

5   Steve Connor, 'Found: the origin of life,' *Independent*, May 14, 2009.

6   If it's so easy that random chemical reactions in a hostile environment can accomplish it, how come decades of sophisticated work by the brightest scientists have been so fruitless?

7   Robert Shapiro in Stephen Benner, Hyo-Joong Kim, and Matthew A. Carrigan, 'Asphalt, Water, and the Prebiotic Synthesis of Ribose, Ribonucleosides, and RNA,' *Accounts of Chemical Research*, vol. 45 (2012) pp. 2025-34.

line of research hasn't made significant advances in the more than 50 years since it was launched.[8]

The second, and perhaps more significant difficulty, is that generating 'letters' is the easiest part in getting an instruction manual. There are many other steps that are nigh impossible without intelligent input.

1. We have to have the letters face the right direction. In biology, R works, but Я doesn't work.

2. The letters have to be attached to each other in the right way. They have to go left to right. You can't stick a letter on top of another letter and have it make sense.

3. Most difficult of all is getting the letters into a meaningful arrangement. The vast majority of random combinations of letters have no meaning:

    a. ouy

    b. oyu

    c. uoy

    d. uyo

---

8   'Origins of life (OOL) research has, to be sure, become progressively more sophisticated, but its goal — to *explain* the origins of life — remains as distant today as it was in 1952. This is not surprising. The protocols in use have remained unchanged: *buy* highly purified chemicals; *mix* them together in high concentrations and in a specific order under carefully devised laboratory conditions; *derive* a mixture of compounds; and *publish* a paper making bold claims about OOL. These protocols are as unrealistic as they are unimproved.' James Tour, 'Time Out,' *Inference*, vol 4 (4 July 2019).

e. you

f. yuo

Of this simple combination of three letters, only one of them has any meaning: 'you.' Similarly, random combinations of 'letters' of RNA or protein mostly have no meaning. Furthermore, the longer the chain of letters, the harder it is to generate a meaningful phrase.[9]

4. Finally, an instruction manual does no good if there's nothing to *read* the manual and follow the instructions.

To show how impossible this is, I routinely conduct a demonstration in my General Biology class. I promise the entire class As for the semester if they can each come up to the front of the class and, one at a time, randomly pick just one Scrabble tile, write it on the board in the order they've picked, and by the end have a meaningful phrase. No class

---

9   For longer sequences it actually becomes exponentially more difficult to randomly generate meaningful phrases. In addition, DNA 'letters' don't 'self-organize' into meaningful combinations any more than English letters self-organize into Shakespeare. 'In particular, a simplified calculation is sufficient to show that the number of distinguishable states of the interactome exceeds comprehension. Consequently, the cell cannot self-organize by random assembly of its components.' Peter Tompa and George Rose, 'The Levinthal Paradox of the Interactome,' *Protein Science* vol. 20 no. 12 (2011) pp. 2074-9.

has ever generated more than a single four-letter word somewhere in the middle of a garbled chain of letters. I'm confident no class ever will since the probability is vanishingly small.

The chance hypothesis for the origin of life faces similar but much harder challenges. DNA, RNA, and protein have to be arranged in the right way, combined in the right way, and make a meaningful sequence that is read and interpreted by something. In our cells, a giant protein called RNA polymerase that's about 3,000 'letters' long reads genetic instructions. Some scientists speculate that it's possible for an RNA sequence to be able to 'read' itself and make more copies of itself. What are the chances of such a thing happening?

The probability of generating a protein 'word' that's 150 letters long by chance has been estimated at 1 in 10^{164}. That's a big number, but just how big? If every single particle in the universe interacted with each other as fast as molecularly possible since the beginning of the known universe, there would be 10^{140} interactions, still 10^{24} away from the probability of a single 150 'letter' long chain. Remember that any actual biological chain capable of the complicated act of self-copying is probably going to have to be much longer than 150 'letters.'

It's possible that one day we may discover a scientific explanation, but that is a statement of faith, not a logical necessity, or even probability. For now, many researchers consider the question 'wide open.'[10] As we gain more and more understanding about how complicated and precise the instructions in cells are, the 'chance' hypothesis faces increasing challenges and becomes less and less satisfactory as an explanation. Origin of life researchers themselves are recognizing the difficulties and asking for more realism in reporting research findings:

> The transformation of an ensemble of appropriately chosen biological monomers (e.g. amino acids, nucleotides) into a primitive living cell capable of further evolution appears to require overcoming an information hurdle of superastronomical proportions, an event that could not have happened within the time frame of the Earth except, we believe, as a miracle. All laboratory experiments attempting to simulate such an event have so far led to dismal failure.[11]

We have, in fact, simplified the challenges here for the sake of brevity. This low probability, nearly miraculous event, would have to be followed by several additional

10 Michael Marshall, 'The Water Paradox and the Origins of Life,' *Nature*, vol. 588 (Dec 2020), pp. 210-13.

11 Edward Steele *et al.*, 'Cause of Cambrian Explosion – Terrestrial or Cosmic?' *Progress in Biophysics and Molecular Biology* vol. 136 (2018), p. 7.

equally low probability events, rendering the whole series probabilistically impossible. In addition to creating a self-replicating information molecule, we would need to simultaneously produce a specialized capsule to protect this molecule (membrane) as well as an efficient and selective means to transport materials through the protective capsule (membrane channels).[12] For example, if we build a machine that prints US currency, we would immediately want to protect it. We can protect it in a hermetically sealed bank vault, but then it does us no good, because it eventually runs out of ink and paper. We need a way to get paper in and keep thieves out. Any original cell would face similar difficulties. In fact, the only uniform and repeatedly experimentally verified mechanism, still in operation today that is known to produce complex, specified information like that seen in DNA and proteins is rational, purposeful intelligence (except that DNA is actually far superior to any kind of language known to humans).[13] The more we unravel the mysteries of DNA, the more marvelous and ingenious it is, bearing all the hallmarks of God's creation.

---

12 There are several other processes that would probably have to appear on the scene simultaneously including information repositories, manufacturing centers, repair systems, and installation processes, to name a few.

13 'DNA is like a computer program but far, far more advanced than any software we've ever created.' Bill Gates, *The Road Ahead* (Viking Press, 1996), p. 228.

SUMMARY OF MAIN POINTS

- Randomly generating the first functional carbon-based informational sequence exceeds the probabilistic resources of our universe.

- There are currently no plausible or even conceivable materialist scenarios for generating the organized, functional informational content necessary for the origin of life.

13

Evolution: The Big Picture

The functional design of organisms and their features would… seem to argue for the existence of a designer. It was Darwin's greatest accomplishment, [however,] to show that the directive organization of living beings can be explained as the result of a natural process, natural selection, without any need to resort to a Creator or other external agent.[1] – Francisco Ayala (Evolutionary Biologist and former Professor at University of California, Irvine)

The fact of evolution is not only inherently atheistic, it is inherently anti-theistic. It goes against the notion that there is a god.[2] – Jerry Coyne (Atheist and University of Chicago Emeritus Professor)

---

1   Richard Dawkins, *The Blind Watchmaker* (W.W. Norton, 1986), p. 1.
2   Jerry Coyne, 'Evolution and atheism: Best friends forever,' *Freethought Today*, Jan/Feb 2017.

A s we've seen, although there are plenty of areas of science that aren't easily explained by purely material explanations, it is the development and complexity of modern biological life that often receives the most attention in this day and age. Darwin's theory of evolution is viewed by many as the final nail in God's coffin.[3]

Evolutionary biologist Ernst Mayr says: 'Explaining the perfection of adaptation by materialistic forces (selection) removed God, so to speak, from his creation. It eliminated the principal arguments of natural theology, and it has been rightly said that natural theology as a viable concept died on November 24, 1859.'[4]

So, let's talk about evolution. Is it really the explanatory panacea for all of biology's complexity problems?

First, what do we mean by 'evolution?' If we mean 'small change and adaptation,' there's little need for any discussion. It's easy to look around us and marvel at the changes and adaptations in the human population or even the vast differences in color, size, and shape we've managed to achieve in the dog population. However, when someone

---

3   A recent survey of college biology students 'found that 56.5% of students perceived that evolution is atheistic.' M. Elizabeth Barnes, Hayley M. Dunlop, Gale M. Sinatra, Taija M. Hendrix, Yi Zheng, Sara E. Brownell, '"Accepting Evolution Means You Can't Believe in God": Atheistic Perceptions of Evolution among College Biology Students,' *CBE – Life Sciences Education*, vol. 19, no. 2 (May 2020)

4   Ernst Mayr, *The Growth of Biological Thought* (Belknap Press, 2003), p. 515.

leaps beyond this kind of word usage, we need to proceed carefully. Dawkins provides an excellent case study:

> Selection – in the form of artificial selection by human breeders – can turn a pye-dog into a Pekinese... in a few centuries. The difference between any two breeds of dog gives us a rough idea of the quantity of evolutionary change that can be achieved in less than a millennium... How many millennia do we have available to us in accounting for the whole history of life?...The time that has elapsed since our fish ancestors crawled out of the water on to the land is about twenty thousand times as long as it took to make all the different...breeds of dogs from the common ancestor that they all share...It becomes rather easy to accept that evolution could accomplish the amount of change that it took to transform a fish into a human.[5]

In this passage, Richard Dawkins conflates two different kinds of evolution: the kind that means small adaptive changes, and the kind that leads to large changes involving new organs and new types of animals. Changes within different kinds of dogs is commonly called 'adaptation' or 'microevolution.' The kind of change that leads from a fish to a dog is commonly called 'macroevolution.' But is there a distinction? Isn't macroevolution just another way of saying 'a whole lot of microevolution?' This is the question we

---

5   Richard Dawkins, *The Greatest Show on Earth* (Free Press, 2009), pp. 81-2.

really need to ask. Can microevolution be extrapolated to macroevolutionary changes?

POSSIBLE EXTRAPOLATIONS

Consider the following scenario:[6]

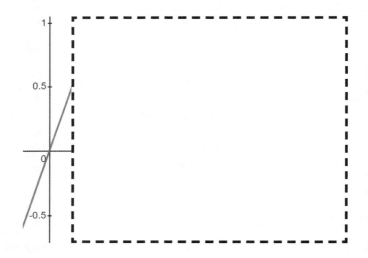

If we were to continue drawing the line into the dashed box where there isn't anything drawn yet, we'd have to extrapolate and make an educated guess about that line. We could easily put a ruler down and guess something like this:

---

6   Graphs generated using Desmos (https://www.desmos.com/calculator).

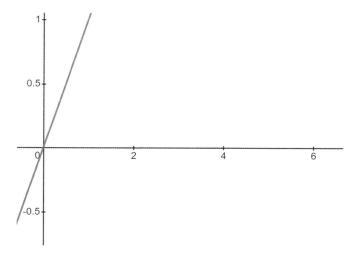

This is a reasonable extrapolation, but it's not the *only* possible line that can be drawn. Our guess is hampered by the fact that we don't know the mathematical equation (the law) that limits and determines the values of this line. Our guess about the line could be wrong. And therefore, it would be unreasonable to overstate our conclusion and say that no other line is possible. What if we knew the equation for the line was y=sin(x), and were shown the actual line?

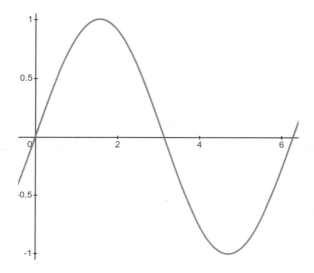

We would be able to see why our guess was wrong and be able to adjust our expectations and predictions for points further along the line. Several different equations reveal different kinds of lines that all have roughly the same starting shape.

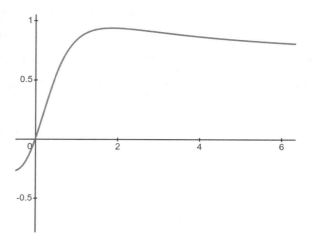

We already intuitively know this kind of thing happens in real life. For example, when we get in our car and press the accelerator, our car speeds up. It is easy for our car to go from 5 mph to 50mph. So, if we just press the accelerator harder, can't we go to 500mph? That seems like a reasonable extrapolation until we think about all of the limiting factors that come into play as we accelerate: aerodynamics of the car, higher frictional forces, upper limits on mechanical rotation of the engine, etc. We can't extrapolate in this way in a linear sense. There are physical limits that we're not aware of at low speeds because they are insignificant, but they play increasingly significant roles at increasingly higher speeds.

Isn't it possible that this is also what's happening with evolutionary change? Certain changes that we can observe empirically have limiting and constraining factors. It was only reasonable to look at microevolution and posit that the adaptive change 'line' extends out forever, growing constantly over time and providing new biological complexity. We've seen organisms change from 5 to 50 in terms of adaptation. Why not go all the way to 500? However, reality could be different. As we do more studying, what if we find that the ability of microevolution to bring about change is limited and encounters a kind of adaptive asymptote that it cannot proceed past?

Almost all of the experimental verification of evolution (thousands of observations, experiments, and studies) has focused only on the early part of the graph (the short line segment I showed in the first picture above). That is the microevolution part that proceeds in a straight line, going upward. We are told repeatedly that evolution has been tested and verified. Textbooks talk about this beginning part of the line and point to experiments in this area as 'overwhelming evidence for evolution.' And, as far as I know, no one disagrees with this part of the graph and the evidence for it. But we're only focusing on this one part of the line. What about the rest of the line? There are other possible lines that could be drawn that also fit the known data.[7] We can't definitively say that our guess is the only right guess if we haven't eliminated other possible lines that fit the data as well. In fact, we'd be overstating our conclusions to say that we know definitively that the line must extend on indefinitely. We can say it's *possible*, but until we have experimental data, nothing is proven and there are many alternative theories that could

---

7   For example, the theistic concept of design provides an equally good explanation for molecular and anatomical homology (similarity) as well as convergent evolution (when unrelated ancestral lines independently arrive at similar design solutions). Conserved/similar genetic material and structures may be God reusing his design template and not the result of evolution at all. For example, humans reuse wheels in multiple kinds of designs.

work. Scientific integrity demands we be honest about the tenuousness of the theorizing at this point.

It's equally likely evolution is like a rubber band around a nail that's stuck in a board. The nail is some kind of organism. The rubber band represents all the different possible adaptations and changes. The rubber band can move all around the nail, going to new places, but as it moves farther away, the rubber band starts really experiencing stretch tension (this would be like the y=sin(x) graph above). The more you move away from the nail, the more tension in the stretch until, ultimately, the rubber band breaks.

Let's take Dawkins' real-world example of dogs. In the few centuries of human breeding of dogs, we've managed to achieve impressive results. We've managed to induce change faster than any kind of natural process could accomplish on its own. Yet, in all that time, we've still only managed to get more dogs. No one has managed to breed something that is 'not dog.' In addition, the more specialized we make these dogs, the more we try to accentuate or highlight particular character traits or physical abilities, the more we 'stretch' the rubber band, the more we introduce weaknesses and problems that make the rubber band want to 'snap back' towards center.

I personally witnessed the impacts of controlled breeding on heritable defects. As a child, I really wanted a dog. My parents encouraged me to do a lot of research on dog demeanors, energy, and size to find the kind of dog that would be happy in our house. I ended up settling for a Shetland sheepdog. After saving up for years, I finally was able to buy a pure-bred Sheltie from a breeder in our area. Shelties are bred for certain qualities, certain looks, hair color, and behavioral traits, but those positive qualities come with weaknesses. We found out later that for some reason, lots of purebred Shelties have gum and teeth issues that other dogs don't have. The same applies for other kinds of dogs: German shepherds are prone to hip dysplasia, huskies autoimmune disorders, poodles glaucoma, cocker spaniels ear infections, etc. The further we 'stretch' the rubber band, the more pressure we apply and the structural 'weaknesses' in the band become apparent. Dogs are a particularly telling case because we've intentionally stretched them further than would happen in the wild with so many competing selective pressures. Most domesticated dogs wouldn't survive in the wild. For all our success, we've really only managed to produce inferior versions of wolves (near the center of the nail). Given enough time in the wild, 'mutts' tend to revert back to a prototypical 'dog-like' state (the rubber band snapping back to the central nail).

MATERIALISTIC EVOLUTIONARY LIMITS

It is one thing to theorize a limit for materialistic evolution, but is there any evidence that such a limit actually exists? It has been proposed that the limit has to do with creating new genetic information. Evolution is great at adapting, varying, altering and modifying *existing* information and structures, but may be unable to *create*. Yet this kind of information creation needs to have happened thousands of times in history if evolution is to explain all of life's complexity.

This problem exists at the molecular level. 'Once you have identified an enzyme [a small protein molecule] that has some weak, promiscuous activity for your target reaction, it's fairly clear that, if you have mutations at random, you can select and improve this activity by several orders of magnitude. What we lack is a hypothesis for the earlier stages, where you don't have this spectrum of enzymatic activities, active sites and folds from which selection can identify starting points. Evolution has this catch-22: Nothing evolves unless it already exists.'[8]

If a purely materialistic, evolutionary view of life is correct, there must be an actual pathway of innovative genetic changes from the first replicating coding material all the way to the complete human genome. Thousands (if not more) individual, creative genetic events must have

---

8 Rajendrani Mukhopadhyay, 'Close to a Miracle,' *ASBMB Today* vol. 12, no. 9 (October 2013), pp. 12-13. See also Douglas Axe and Ann Gauger, 'Model and Laboratory Demonstrations That Evolutionary Optimization Works Well Only If Preceded by Invention – Selection Itself Is Not Inventive,' *BIO-Complexity*, vol. 2(2015), pp. 1-13.

occurred over the history of life. From a purely numeric standpoint, our genome is billions of base pairs which are orders of magnitude larger than the first organism, so we must have added information somewhere along the way. So, our question for anyone who believes evolution is capable of 'extending the line' to make new organs and complex systems is: **Can you show experimental evidence for the purely materialistic, unguided creation of a multistep molecular innovation that uses new genetic information?**

What are we asking here? Imagine a large sound board with lots of dials, knobs and sliders. On a soundboard, turning a dial might increase the bass or fine-tune a particular treble frequency. Each dial could represent a gene in our genome. Turning a dial is a lot like making changes to gene expression or like simple mutations that we can easily see in adaptations in humans and other organisms. We can 'tune' the gene to cause changes in output. We can create lots of different sounds by changing knobs and dials, similar to how we can create lots of differences in organisms through genetic changes. But the question remains: how did the knobs and dials get on the board in the first place? In biological terms, is there experimental evidence that evolution is capable of creating a 'knob,' and not just adjusting and tuning the 'knobs' once they're already there?

It's unreasonable to expect a detailed molecular explanation for every innovative pathway since the beginning of time, but we would expect to see experimental vindication of at least one. In other words, we're requesting proof of concept. This innovative step is a significant and necessary pillar in the evolutionary story. If it's not possible, then at the very least a major overhaul is in order. If someone told us they had invented a small handheld device that allows us to fly, we'd probably want to see some actual test runs before we trusted it. Even seeing detailed blueprints wouldn't be enough. We would need an actual, real world trial. Similarly, we want to see some evidence for this particular evolutionary step before we could consider it trustworthy (not just descriptions, simulations, or models).

To date, there is not a single demonstrated example of this kind of unguided innovation. This is incredibly striking! We've been studying this for decades, with our knowledge base growing almost exponentially year-by-year, and we still have not discovered one example of an experimentally verified chance-based molecular innovation with new genetic material. It may be that someday someone will discover such a thing, but until then we shouldn't accept a purely materialist evolutionary theory that can't be shown to produce even one example of what it needs to produce. Many already recognize this same shortcoming:

> There is no publication in the scientific literature – in prestigious journals, specialty journals, or books – that describes how molecular evolution of any real,

complex, biochemical system either did occur, or even might have occurred.[9]

[T]here are presently no detailed Darwinian accounts of the evolution of any biochemical or cellular system, only a variety of wishful speculations.[10]

In fact, to our knowledge, no macromutations ... that gave birth to novel proteins have yet been identified.[11]

... over the broad sweep of evolutionary time what we would really like to explain is the gain of complexity and the origins of novel adaptations.[12]

It is not clear how natural selection can operate in the origin of folds or active site architecture (of proteins). It is equally unclear how either micromutations or macromutations could repeatedly and reliably lead to large evolutionary transitions. What remains is a deep, tantalizing, perhaps immovable mystery.[13]

9   John Lennox, *God's Undertaker* (Lion Hudson, 2009), p. 124.

10 Franklin M. Harold, *The Way of the Cell: Molecules, Organisms, and the Order of Life* (Oxford University Press, 2001), p. 205.

11 Ágnes Tóth-Petróczy and Dan S. Tawfik, 'Hopeful (Protein InDel) Monsters?' *Structure* vol. 22 (2014), p. 803.

12 Nicola J. Nadeau and Chris D. Jiggins, 'A Golden Age for Evolutionary Genetics? Genomic Studies of Adaptation in Natural Populations,' *Trends in Genetics* vol. 26 (2010), pp. 484-92.

13 Tyler Hampton, 'Dan S. Tawfik Group: The New View of Proteins,' *Inference* vol. 1, no. 1 (October 2014).

SUMMARY OF MAIN POINTS

- There is considerable scientific evidential support for the ability of organisms to display very limited variation and adaptation within specific bounds through alterations in existing genetic information, frequently through deletions or changes in expression.

- No experimental evidence currently exists that demonstrates how unguided processes can generate the genetic information necessary for entirely new biological structures.

14

Evolution: Darwin's Defenders

The ideas we've presented are not new, and there have been a variety of responses from scientists and non-scientists alike, some more cogent than others. In what follows, I will present some of the most common rebuttals. From the outset, I need to point out that these are not meant to be comprehensive, but rather representative. I cannot lay out in detail every argument against my position any more than I can lay out every argument for my position. If the details do interest you, I'd encourage you to check out the lively and ongoing dialogue that exists among the experts by referencing some of the materials in the Appendix. There are links to a few websites that demonstrate some actual back-and-forth discussions as opposed to a one-sided monologue.

APPEAL TO AUTHORITY

Perhaps one of the least compelling arguments, but one that comes up quite frequently, is the logical fallacy called the 'appeal to authority.' This occurs when someone claims, 'there is no controversy,' 'the overwhelming scientific consensus supports,' 'certainty not in question,' or 'every scientist I know agrees.' Just because many scientists believe materialistic evolution to be true, does not make it so. Scientists are experts and they've performed lots of experiments, and spent lots of time thinking about this, but scientists can be (and have been) wrong. [1] We should take scientific claims seriously and afford them proper respect, but they're not perfect. Geocentrism again provides an instructive example here. Just a few hundred years ago, there was no controversy and the vast amount of empirical evidence supported the scientific consensus that the earth was the center of the solar system. Scientists were wrong. There are other examples in the history of science; thus we

---

1   However, the vast majority of scientists are not experts in evolution specifically and are inclined to defer to a (relatively) small number of evolutionary biologists thus potentially inflating the consensus numbers. It's a little like asking someone if they think baseball is the world's greatest sport and they respond, 'Well, I don't know much about sports, so I asked a professional baseball player and he said baseball is the best sport, and I'm inclined to agree.' See also Allen, Jarred & Lay, Cindy & Montanez, George, 'A Castro Consensus: Understanding the Role of Dependence in Consensus Formation' *Conference of Truth and Trust Online* (2020).

must be cautious about concluding that truth is determined by a majority vote.

DENIAL OF ALTERNATIVE HYPOTHESES

Some people will claim that materialist evolutionary theory is the only game in town. Nothing else works and science would collapse without Darwinism. 'Nothing in biology makes sense except in the light of evolution.'[2]

Though this could be true, it could also represent an unwillingness to seriously consider and examine other hypotheses. As we've tried to point out, much of the existing evidence can be explained by an intelligent, designing Creator. For example, anatomical and molecular homology and convergence match what we would expect from design theory. Failure to consider a designing God, for personal or metaphysical reasons, would not be scientific.

Furthermore, if it is true that materialistic evolutionary explanations for complex life are inadequate, would biology collapse? This seems improbable considering the number of biologists for whom evolution is unnecessary or irrelevant to their work.

> [O]ver the last 100 years, almost all of biology has proceeded independent of evolution, except evolutionary biology itself. Molecular biology,

---

2 Theodosius Dobzhansky, 'Nothing in biology makes sense except in the light of evolution,' *American Biology Teacher*, vol. 35, no. 3 (1973), pp. 125-9.

biochemistry, and physiology, have not taken evolution into account at all.[3]

I also examined the outstanding biodiscoveries of the past century: the discovery of the double helix; the characterization of the ribosome; the mapping of genomes; research on medications and drug reactions; improvements in food production and sanitation; the development of new surgeries; and others... Here, as elsewhere, I found that Darwin's theory had provided no discernible guidance, but was brought in, after the breakthroughs, as an interesting narrative gloss.[4]

Content experts are more likely to become entrenched in their beliefs and fail to adequately recognize reasonable alternatives. As David Epstein, author of *Range: Why Generalists Triumph in a Specialized World* observes, 'When entire specialties grow up around devotion to a particular tool, the result can be disastrous myopia.'[5]

STORYTELLING AND IMAGINATION

We are drawn to stories. There is a huge market for novels and movies that tell excellent stories. They lead us one small step at a time to a grand climax and conclusion. We have

3   Marc Kirschner, quoted in Peter Dizikes, 'Missing Links,' *The Boston Globe*, October 23, 2005.

4   Philip Skell, 'Why Do We Invoke Darwin?' *The Scientist*, August 28, 2005.

5   David Epstein, *Range: Why Generalists Triumph in a Specialized World* (Riverhead, 2019), p. 265.

learned in everything from advertising to schoolwork, that a coherent story is enticing. We want to believe stories, particularly when they're just on the edge of plausibility. But a story can be true or false.

Growing up, I read Rudyard Kipling's *Just So Stories* that were whimsical, make-believe stories about how certain biological traits came into existence, such as 'How the Camel Got His Hump' and 'How the Leopard Got His Spots.' As the Wikipedia article helpfully summarizes, 'In science and philosophy, a just-so story is an unverifiable narrative explanation for a cultural practice, a biological trait, or behavior of humans or other animals. The pejorative nature of the expression is an implicit criticism that reminds the hearer of the essentially fictional and unprovable nature of such an explanation.'[6]

For instance, imagine a horse developed a protuberance of keratin (similar to what makes up hooves) on the top of its head. This visible protuberance helped it identify similar species and served a secondary function as a display for mate selection. Over time the protuberance sharpened and helped the horse fend off predators as well as win dominance fights with other males over females. Thus, we have a plausible adaptive pathway to the modern day unicorn! Obviously,

---

6   https://en.wikipedia.org/wiki/Just-so_story

this story isn't true, yet this is similar to the story you'll see for how some animals (like rhinos) get tusks or horns.

Unfortunately, this kind of fanciful storytelling is encouraged in schools and tends to be more the rule than the exception among many scientists. Although stating a plausible scenario can provide the scientific community with potential avenues for investigation, stating a 'just-so' story as fact is misleading. One scientist recently stated, 'This paper explains how the antifreeze protein in the northern codfish evolved.'[7] When you actually read the paper, however, there is no experiment showing how it evolved, just a series of hypotheses, guesses and suggestions at a potential route. It's not even clear there are hypotheses for all the necessary steps: 'somehow, the gene also obtained the proper control sequence.'[8] So, scientists, too, are prone to 'just-so' stories. We just make them sound more technical.

We are too easily persuaded to fill in gaps in knowledge with vibrant storytelling. It's human nature, and materialistic evolution excels at this kind of storytelling.[9] By arranging

7   Christina Cheng, quoted in University of Illinois, 'Study of Arctic fishes reveals the birth of a gene – from junk,' *Phys.org* February 11, 2019.

8   Ibid.

9   One study suggests that storytelling is the most effective way to get students to understand evolution. Buchan, L., Hejmadi, M., Abrahams, L. *et al.* 'A RCT for assessment of active human-centred learning finds teacher-centric non-human teaching of evolution optimal.' *npj Science of Learning* vol 5, no. 19 (2020).

pieces the right way, we can tell almost any story we want. Drawing pictures or lining up fossils doesn't mean there's an actual flow from one to the other. You can line up a series of cars from a Volkswagen Bug to a Formula One race car, but that doesn't mean such a transition happens naturally without any help. Almost anything is possible, but is it true? A story by itself doesn't constitute a sufficient rejoinder to the information innovation challenge I've posed.

In addition, fanciful stories are flexible and can be molded to fit any narrative outcome. Because of the adaptability of stories, it can be difficult to prove one wrong. A recent post at *Nature* concedes: 'Once fortified with historical inertia, just-so stories are difficult to interrogate.'[10] We see this with large-scale evolutionary theory which has very little predictive power but can be made to explain (after the fact) even contradictory and opposing data. For example, the discovery of large, non-functional 'junk DNA' sequences was heralded as evidence of the scars of millennia of mutations and evolutionary tinkering. When the opposite was later found to be true (most of these sequences turned out to have important functions), the evolutionary story was adapted to fit the new data. The high functionality of DNA

---

10   Tetsuto Miyashita, 'Agnatha All Along? Changing the Evolutionary Narrative of Vertebrate Origins.' *Nature Ecology and Evolution*, (March 17, 2021).

was now evidence of the efficiency and parsimoniousness of evolution.[11]

This is why we emphasized *experimental evidence* in our initial question to scientists. If someone shows a picture series of transitional organisms or tells a plausible story of something that happened 'one small change at a time,' we should ask for the details. What changed? What gene and what mutation within that gene? A 'plausible' story about a gene changing won't suffice either. Where is the experimental evidence, not just anecdotal? 'If intermediate steps are not enumerated and tested for a physical pathway, then a theorist is in serious danger of getting stuck in a fantasy world.'[12]

In the few cases where we have undertaken experiments to test the validity of these stories, they've fallen flat: 'We tested a widely held hypothesis of molecular adaptation—that changes in the alcohol dehydrogenase protein (ADH) along the lineage leading to *Drosophila melanogaster* increased the catalytic activity of the enzyme and thereby contributed to the ethanol tolerance and adaptation of the species to its ethanol-rich ecological niche. Our experiments strongly refute the predictions of the adaptive ADH hypothesis and caution against accepting intuitively appealing accounts of

11   For more on this, see Jonathan Wells, *The Myth of Junk DNA* (Discovery Institute Press, 2011).

12   Michael Behe, 'Philosophical-ish Objections to Intelligent Design: A Response to Paul Draper,' *Evolution News*, February 19, 2020.

historical molecular adaptation that are based on correlative evidence. The experimental strategy we employed can be used to decisively test other adaptive hypotheses and the claims they entail about past biological causality.'[13]

Once you start digging, it's astonishing how devoid of details the literature is in this regard. Once you know to look for these evolutionary 'just-so' stories, you'll start seeing them everywhere! In the literature, examples of genetic innovation are only ever described as speculative stories. Check out this admission from the editorial introducing a whole issue focused on cellular evolution:

> The evolutionary history of the cell is shrouded in a past so distant and deep it has left few tangible traces of what early cells might have looked like and which processes may have gone on inside them. Hence, the study of cellular evolutionary history relies largely on inference. These inferences center on phylogenetic frameworks built with extant cells. Their traits are compared, and what we know about their biology is projected into the past. Phylogenetic trees are calibrated and constrained by fossils and geological events so that a sequence of evolutionary transitions can be inferred. Naturally, speculation and contention abound—which is part of the charm of this field.[14]

---

13 Siddiq, M., Loehlin, D., Montooth, K. *et al.* 'Experimental test and refutation of a classic case of molecular adaptation in *Drosophila melanogaster*,' *National Ecology and Evolution* vol 1, no. 25 (2017).

14 Florian Maderspacher, 'The long dark teatime of the cell,' *Current Biology* vol. 30, no. 10(May 18, 2020), PR451-R453.

In other words, the actual significant evolutionary changes are based on guesses, not lab experiments.

Interestingly, Christianity doesn't suffer from the same explanatory storytelling issues because we don't claim God uses purely materialistic means. We don't claim that there must exist an actual, traceable genetic lineage.

ADAPTIVE LOSS OF FUNCTION

There are several examples in biology of some organisms gaining adaptive advantage over other organisms due to gene changes. Although these changes look innovative and drastic at the surface level, when we probe the molecular level, these are frequently 'loss of function' changes, which are going the opposite direction of what we need to show biologically. This is why our question emphasizes examples of *new* genetic information.

For example, you can sometimes make a book read more smoothly or even change the meaning of a passage by deleting sentences or paragraphs. However, this loss of information doesn't help introduce new sentences and paragraphs that are what is necessary to get a book in the first place. In order to delete a sentence, someone had to write the sentence to begin with. The question we are asking is: Can evolution *create* biological sentences, not just improve an organism by deleting sentences? Thus, this kind of 'loss of function' adaptation (where an organism 'improves' by deleting existing material – a frequent strategy in antibiotic resistance[15]) doesn't meet the standard to answer our question. This is why it's important, when someone points to a supposed counter-example, to examine what's actually happening at the molecular level. 'When people saw a mutation that helped, they confused *beneficial* mutations with *constructive* mutations.'[16] That is, just because something is adaptive and helpful in the moment, doesn't mean you've created something new or generated new information.

Perhaps a more tangible analogy would be helpful here. We can improve a car's speed by lightening the load and tossing out the seats, the rugs, and the spare tire, but have we improved the car overall? We have introduced a change to the car that is beneficial, with respect to speed, but is not constructive with respect to content/information. Once those things are gone, we can't get them back, or at least not easily. So it is with many organisms, especially bacteria: they

15   Interestingly, by understanding the constraints on the evolution of antibiotic resistance, we may be able to figure out how to overcome that very resistance. Maeda, T., Iwasawa, J., Kotani, H. *et al.* 'High-throughput laboratory evolution reveals evolutionary constraints in *Escherichia coli.*' *Nature Communications* vol 11, no. 5970 (2020).

16   Michael Behe, 'Darwinism's big breakdown,' *WORLD magazine* vol 34, no. 23 (December 7, 2019), pp. 40-1.

can 'improve' one aspect by damaging themselves genetically in another way.[17]

For something like macroevolution to be true, we must be able to show that it can create new structures and new architecture, not just deconstruct and rearrange what's already there. We are back to the 'nothing evolves unless it already exists' problem.

'In laboratory-based experimental evolution of novel phenotypes and the human domestication of crops, the majority of the mutations that lead to adaptation are loss-of-function mutations that impair or eliminate the function of genes rather than gain-of-function mutations that increase or qualitatively alter the function of proteins. Here, I speculate that easier access to loss-of-function mutations has led them to play a major role in the adaptive radiations that occur when populations have access to many unoccupied ecological niches.'[18] This kind of adaptive change is attractive and contributes to a lot of variation, but doesn't solve our problem of how to get new information in the first place.

OTHER EXAMPLES OF MOLECULAR INNOVATION

In the literature there have been several supposed examples of genuine molecular innovation. However, upon further

17 For more, see Michael Behe, *Darwin Devolves* (HarperOne, 2019).
18 Andrew Murray, 'Can gene-inactivating mutations lead to evolutionary novelty?' *Current Biology* vol. 30, no. 10 (May 18, 2020), R465-R471.

inspection they all fail to adequately answer the question at hand. One example of this kind of thing was the discovery of an enzyme called nylonase in bacteria that breaks down nylon. Since nylon is a relatively recent synthetic human invention not found in nature, scientists were understandably excited about such a discovery. It turned out however that the enzyme in its naturally pre-existing form *already* happened to have weak promiscuous nylonase activity and just adapted to improve that ability: it evolved what already existed.[19]

Perhaps one of the most interesting experiments is Richard Lenski's Long-Term Evolutionary Experiment (LTEE) with bacteria. He has carefully tracked and monitored changes in *E.Coli* bacteria for more than 70,000 generations, which is roughly 1.5 million years in human generations. For perspective, modern scientists say human-like creatures have only been around for about 6 million years and our particular species (Homo sapiens) about 300,000 years. So, in terms of generations, he's been tracking changes in this population of bacteria for longer than we as a species have been around.

---

19 S. Negoro et al., 'X-ray Crystallographic Analysis of 6-Aminohexanoate-Dimer Hydrolase: Molecular Basis for the Birth of a Nylon Oligomer-Degrading Enzyme,' *Journal of Biological Chemistry* vol. 280, no. 47 (November 25, 2005), pp. 39644-52.

To date, he hasn't found a single molecular innovation that fits our criteria.

To be fair, Lenski's experiments aren't designed to perfectly mimic *actual* evolution, but those results are still telling. Given the number of innovative creative changes that would have been necessary to get humans, and the fact that we haven't observed *a single one* in his bacteria, that should at least give us pause to consider if materialistic evolution really has the power to deliver all it has promised.[20]

But what about real nature? What about changes in the wild with all kinds of selective pressures and a range of available tools for organisms to use? 'A survey of all known malarial evolutionary responses to human drugs includes *no* novel protein-protein interactions. Since widespread drug treatments first appeared about fifty years ago, more than

---

20 What has Lenski found? A number of genes changed their levels of expression (meaning they changed amounts of existing proteins – no new information). Several adaptive 'loss of function' mutations were identified (loss of genetic information). A single strain developed the ability to consume citrate, which sounds exciting, but, after further investigation, it turned out the bacteria *already* had this ability, it was just normally suppressed (no new information). Interestingly, before the true cause of the citrate ability was discovered, this citrate-eating bacteria was initially lauded as the proof that had been missing – highlighting that this is indeed a big hole in evolutionary theory: 'A major innovation has unfurled right in front of researchers' eyes. It's the first time evolution has been caught in the act of making such a rare and complex new trait.' Bob Holmes, 'Bacteria make major evolutionary shift in the lab,' *New Scientist*, (June 9, 2008).

10^{20}, a hundred billion billion, malarial cells have been born in infested regions. It thus appears that the likelihood of the development of a new, useful, specific protein-protein interaction is less than one in 10^{20}.'[21] In other words, in a real-world situation with all kinds of selective pressures, and over an incredible number of generations, evolution has failed to produce the kind of protein change we're asking for. These same numbers, observations, and conclusions roughly apply for the AIDS virus as well.

We must be careful not to overstate the conclusions here, but Lenski's experiment and attempts by others have as of yet failed to provide evidence of evolution-based genetic innovation.[22] Honestly, I'm not holding my breath.

OTHER SOURCES OF GENETIC INNOVATION

Are there any other potential ways to generate genetic innovation? What about things like gene duplication and divergence, or exaptation (change of function)?

There are several things that can be said about these, but the counter-arguments miss the mark for many of the same reasons previous arguments did. Anyone can propose a number of plausible ways to fly to other solar systems in a lifetime, but none have been observed or experimentally

---

21 Michael Behe, *The Edge of Evolution* (Free Press, 2007), p. 136.

22 Mutations in the *ebg* gene in *E.Coli*, *TRIM5* in owl monkeys, and Cichlid populations were loudly proclaimed as innovative, but ended up just being alterations of existing information.

verified. Similarly, anyone can propose a number of plausible ways to generate new genetic innovation, but none of them have been observed or experimentally verified. We're back to storytelling again.

In terms of exaptation: '[W]e might think that some of the parts of a …complex system evolved step by step for some other purpose and were then recruited wholesale to a new function. But this is also unlikely. You may as well hope that half your car's transmission will suddenly help out in the airbag department. Such things might happen very, very rarely, but they surely do not offer a general solution to … complexity.'[23]

Gene duplication with subsequent accumulation of mutations is the explanation of choice for most, if not all, proteins where scientists believe they know something about how the protein originated. However, whenever you need more than a few amino acid changes in your protein sequence, research indicates materialistic evolutionary processes may not be up to the task.[24] Experiments show that gene duplications accumulate deletions and loss of function

---

23 H. Allen Orr, 'Darwin v. intelligent design (again),' *Boston Review* (Dec/Jan 1996), pp. 28-31.

24 Michael Behe, *Darwin Devolves* (HarperOne, 2019), pp. 213-5.

mutations at an incredible rate making this suggestion incredibly improbable.[25]

Stephen Meyer discusses gene duplications and it's worth quoting him at length: 'The papers in the primary literature that do talk about gene duplication and the changes that would have to happen afterwards fail to demonstrate *how* mutations and natural selection could find truly novel genes or proteins in sequence space in the first place; nor do they show that it is reasonably probable (or plausible) that these mechanisms would do so in the time available. These papers *assume* the existence of significant amounts of *preexisting* genetic information (indeed, many whole and unique genes) and then *suggest* various mechanisms that might have slightly altered or fused these genes together into larger composites. At best, these scenarios "trace" the history of preexisting genes, rather that *explain* the origin of the original genes themselves.'[26]

---

25 In addition, gene duplication creates more information, but not *new* information. The same problem applies to exon shuffling, retropositioning of mRNA transcripts, lateral gene transfer, transfer of mobile genetic units, rewiring of developmental gene regulatory networks, and gene fission or fusion. For an estimate of some of the probabilities see Michael Behe and David Snoke 'Simulating evolution by gene duplication of protein features that require multiple amino acid residues,' *Protein Science*, vol. 13, no. 10 (October 2004), pp. 2651–64.

26 Stephen Meyer, *Darwin's Doubt* (HarperOne, 2013), p. 212. 'Gene duplication and loss is a powerful source of functional innovation. However, the general principles that govern this process are still

Meyer continues, 'Overall, what evolutionary biologists have in mind is something like trying to produce a new book by copying the pages of an existing book (gene duplication, lateral gene transfer, and transfer of mobile genetic elements), rearranging blocks of text on each page (exon shuffling, retropositioning, and gene fusion), making random spelling changes to words in each block of text (point mutations), and then randomly rearranging the new pages. Clearly, such random rearrangements and changes will have no realistic chance of generating a literary masterpiece, let alone a coherent read.'[27]

Even non-theistic scientists are beginning to doubt that standard Darwinian theory is sufficiently explanatory. This statement from the Royal Society is revealing:

> A rising number of publications argue for a major revision or even a replacement of the standard theory of evolution, indicating that this cannot be dismissed as a minority view but rather is a widespread feeling among scientists and philosophers alike...For instance, the theory largely avoids the question of how the complex organizations of organismal structure, physiology, development or behavior — whose variation it describes — actually arise in evolution... The real issue is that genetic evolution alone has been

---

largely unknown.' Wapinski, I., Pfeffer, A., Friedman, N. *et al.* 'Natural history and evolutionary principles of gene duplication in fungi.' *Nature* vol. 449, (2007) pp. 54-61.

27 Ibid., p. 219.

found insufficient for an adequate causal explanation
of all forms of phenotypic complexity, not only of
something vaguely termed 'macroevolution.'[28]

Although these scientists haven't abandoned evolution (they
call for something known as the Extended Evolutionary
Synthesis or EES), they are at least admitting that there are
problems and unanswered questions. Why don't we hear
more about this? It may be at least partly because they're
afraid that admitting weakness might mean the idea of God
as designer could gain ground. 'Yet the mere mention of
the EES often evokes an emotional, even hostile, reaction
among evolutionary biologists. Too often, vital discussions
descend into acrimony, with accusations of muddle or
misrepresentation. Perhaps haunted by the specter of
intelligent design, evolutionary biologists wish to show a
united front.'[29] It seems that some scientists keep the tenuous
reality of the situation quiet for personal and theological
reasons, not scientific.

28 Gerd B. Muller, 'Why an Extended Evolutionary Synthesis Is
    Necessary,' *Interface Focus* vol. 7 (2017) 20170015.

29 Kevin Laland, Tobias Uller, Marc Feldman, Kim Sterelny, Gerd
    B. Müller, Armin Moczek, Eva Jablonka, and John Odling-Smee,
    'Does evolutionary theory need a rethink? Yes, urgently,' *Nature*,
    vol. 514 (October, 2014) pp. 161-4.

ARGUMENT FROM IGNORANCE

Just because we haven't found experimental evidence for a genetically innovative pathway doesn't mean such a thing doesn't exist. This is true, but it also doesn't mean such a pathway *does* exist and that we will find it. We should lend more credence to alternative explanations that *do* fit the known data. The more time passes without the necessary evidence, the more the case for purely materialistic evolutionary pathways looks increasingly desperate. This is *unless* there exists a pre-determined commitment to materialism that refuses to acknowledge that God is involved in His creation. But then we've crossed from being good scientists to making blind faith, philosophical assumptions without evidence.

The math for a genetically innovative pathway makes for fantastical odds. Several peer-reviewed scientific papers have estimated the odds of creating a new protein, or new protein fold, at less than 1 in 10^{60}.[30] The odds could be as

30 Hubert Yockey, 'A calculation of the probability of spontaneous biogenesis by information theory,' *Journal of Theoretical Biology* vol. 67, no. 3 (August 7, 1977), pp. 377-398; JF Reidhaar-Olson, RT Sauer, 'Functionally acceptable substitutions in two alpha-helical regions of lambda repressor,' *Proteins*, vol. 7, no. 4 (1990) pp. 306-16; Yuuki Hayashi, Takuyo Aita, Hitoshi Toyota, Itaru Urabe, Tetsuya Yomo, 'Experimental Rugged Fitness Landscape in Protein Sequence Space,' *PLOS One* (December 20, 2006).

infinitesimally small as 1 in $10^{10^{18}}$.[31] (For comparison, there are about 10^{80} atoms in the entire universe.)

One common rejoinder is that the probability of any complex, specified sequence is always low, yet it happens. For example, let's say I dealt you a hand of five poker cards. You get a 3, 6, 8, 9 and Queen, all of clubs. The probability of drawing this specific hand is 1 in 2,598,960. Yet, as improbable as it seems, this is the hand you were dealt! What's going on here? It turns out the probability of drawing *any* specific hand in poker is always 1 in 2,598,960. In the poker game you're playing, the probability of drawing some hand is 100%, but if you were to attempt to guess *ahead of time* what your hand would be, you'd only have a 1 in 2,598,960 chance of being correct.

So, how does this connect to our protein example? The argument says that the probability of a specific protein sequence *picked ahead of time* is very small, but the probability of some sequence is very large (possibly 100%), thus we shouldn't be surprised that some sequence is picked.

But is this true? Yes, we could randomly generate a new protein sequence, but that doesn't mean the sequence would work. In poker, you have a 100% chance of drawing a hand of cards, but what's the chance that your hand of cards will

---

31 Eugene Koonin, 'The cosmological model of eternal inflation and the transition from chance to biological evolution in the history of life,' *Biology Direct* vol. 2, no. 15 (2007).

win the round? In biology, not just any protein sequence will work. We need to know how many working protein sequences there are out of all possible sequences in order to estimate the probability of 'being dealt' a working sequence. In poker you'd need to know what cards your opponent has in order to know the probability of being dealt a hand that will beat him. This difficulty is called the combinatorial problem.[32]

In biology these odds are extremely low. It would be like drawing a royal flush millions of times in a row – at which point would you really believe it's random and unguided? Some scientists have estimated that only one in 10^{60} or 10^{70} randomly generated protein sequences would form a working protein domain (for reference, there are only about 10^{80} atoms in the whole universe and only about 10^{40} organisms have ever existed in the history of this planet).[33] In attempting to convert a functional protein fold into a

---

32 For a more detailed discussion see Stephen Meyer, *Return of the God Hypothesis: Three Scientific Discoveries That Reveal the Mind Behind the Universe'* (HarperOne, 2021), pp. 205-7.

33 Douglas Axe, 'Estimating the Prevalence of Protein Sequences Adopting Functional Enzyme Folds,' *Journal of Molecular Biology* vol. 341, no. 5 (August 27, 2004), pp. 1295-315. See also Sean Taylor et al., 'Searching Sequence Space for Protein Catalysts,' *Proceedings of the National Academy of Sciences USA* vol. 98 (2001) pp. 10596-601; K.K. Durston et al., 'Measuring the Functional Sequence Complexity of Proteins,' *Theoretical Biology and Medical Modelling* vol. 4 (2007) pp. 47.

new and different fold, you are much more likely to destroy it.[34]

COMMON DESCENT AND HUMAN ORIGINS

I think it useful to close by briefly discussing common descent and the uniqueness of humans. I'm keeping it brief because we actually know very little. Non-Christian materialists assume Darwinian evolution is true and therefore assume that humans arose as a population of individuals from ape-like ancestors. If these assumptions are correct, the classic Biblical concept of Adam and Eve cannot be true. However, these assumptions haven't really been tested. It's a little like watching a group of people changing a light bulb and then always assuming it requires a group without ever testing to see if one person can do it. Until recently, no one had bothered looking to see if it was possible that we came from a single parental unit. In the last several years, genetic analysis has indicated that it is possible, and consistent with our present understanding of science, that we came from a single parentage.[35] Thus, the classic Christian understanding of Adam and Eve does fit with the scientific data.

---

34 Nobuhiko Tokuriki and Dan Tawfik, 'Stability Effects of Mutations and Protein Evolvability,' *Current Opinion in Structural Biology* vol. 19 no. 5 (2009) pp. 596-604.

35 Ola Hössjer and Ann Gauger, A Single-Couple Human Origin is Possible,' *BIO-Complexity* vol. 1 (2019), pp. 1-20. See also Ann Gauger, Douglas Axe, Casey Luskin, *Science & Human Origins* (Discovery Institute Press, 2012).

To wrap up this section on evolution and biological complexity, we should acknowledge that God can leave His identifiable mark by using secondary causes to accomplish His purposes. The Bible gives several examples of God using 'natural' things like weather and animals in particular ways for a particular purpose (see Exod. 7-10). Natural theologian William Paley puts it this way:

> If, in tracing these causes, it be said, that we find certain general properties of matter, which have nothing in them that bespeaks intelligence, I answer, that, still, the managing of these properties, the pointing and directing them to the uses which we see made of them, demands intelligence in the highest degree.... There may be many second causes, and many courses of second causes, one behind another, between what we observe of nature and the Deity; but there must be intelligence somewhere; there must be more in nature than what we see; and, amongst the things unseen, there must be an intelligent, designing author.[36]

If you were to look at a car assembly line, the whole thing runs on its own with each machine doing its part in the process to create a final product. However, everyone knows that the whole process, including each of the machines along the way, was designed and created by intelligent engineers and scientists. Similarly, the cell is a factory that acquires,

---

36   William Paley, *Natural Theology* (Oxford University Press, 2008), p. 218.

converts and uses energy for its operation. Might it not be the most intelligently designed factory ever made?

Award-winning biologist Bruce Alberts describes the cell this way: 'But instead of a cell dominated by randomly colliding individual protein molecules, we now know that nearly every major process in a cell is carried out by assemblies of 10 or more protein molecules. And, as it carries out its biological functions, each of these protein assemblies interacts with several other large complexes of proteins. Indeed, the entire cell can be viewed as a factory that contains an elaborate network of interlocking assembly lines, each of which is composed of a set of large protein machines... Why do we call the large protein assemblies that underlie cell function protein *machines*? Precisely because, like the machines invented by humans to deal efficiently with the macroscopic world, these protein assemblies contain highly coordinated moving parts. Within each protein assembly, intermolecular collisions are not only restricted to a small set of possibilities, but reaction C depends on reaction B, which in turn depends on reaction A—just as it would in a machine of our common experience.'[37] Alberts has, perhaps unwittingly, put forth an apt description of God's molecular machines!

---

37   Bruce Alberts, 'The Cell as a Collection of Protein Machines: Preparing the Next Generation of Molecular Biologists,' *Cell* vol. 92, no. 3 (February, 1998), pp. 291-4.

I realize that this chapter has covered some technical scientific points that aren't always easy for non-specialists to grasp, so let me briefly summarize. Hopefully you can see that the issues and questions surrounding evolution are a bit thornier than have been publicly advertised. It's possible that there is an 'upper limit' for evolutionary adaptation at the level of generating complicated genetic innovation for new biological structures. Thankfully the scientific enterprise continues unabated and time will show whether this is an insurmountable hurdle for materialistic macroevolution.

SUMMARY OF MAIN POINTS

- Most counterarguments fall into one of several categories: an appeal to authority or consensus, fanciful, imaginary storytelling of 'possible scenarios,' adaptations that improve fitness (but not by genetic innovation), or suggestions of possible genetic mechanisms that have not been experimentally verified.

- Current genetic analyses suggest that humans could all be descended from a single pair of humans, as the Bible indicates.

Conclusion

By examining both the scientific method, the scientific evidence, and the assumptions that underlie our use of evidence, we've come to see that modern science tacitly depends on Christian presuppositions. Christianity is well supported by the existing evidence, helping to explain how and why the world is the way it is. Furthermore, Christianity is an internally consistent and coherent worldview since its beliefs and assumptions fully support one another without contradiction.

It is worth pointing out here at the end, that although Biblical Christianity matches what we know from science, that doesn't mean all our questions are answered. It can be difficult to wrap our minds around it, but if Christianity is true we should *expect* to find mysterious things that we can't fully fathom. God, to be really God, should have understanding that surpasses our creaturely, finite minds. There is a place for mystery, wonder and undefinable awe in a Christian's life in the world of science.

Wanting to know and understand creation is good, but to think we can know and explain everything is the pinnacle of human hubris. This is an underlying assumption sneaked into materialist versions of science: 'I want to know.' 'I need to know.' 'I deserve to know.' What's so wrong with not knowing? What's wrong with humbly admitting what we don't know, and choosing to glorify and praise God? This doesn't mean we stop *trying* to know, but it does give us a proper perspective on the pursuit of knowledge.[1]

It should come as no surprise we can have such a huge problem with the mystery of God. The world has told us our whole lives that we can do, become, or know whatever we want. Supposedly, there are no limits. We are god-like. And if you start by saying there can be no mystery, then there can be no God. The existence of mystery is a reminder of our place in this world: we are not God. We don't have all the answers, although we trust that He does. Yet, because we are made by God in His image, we are driven by curiosity and an unquenchable desire to know Him, in His Word and in His creation. In that search and desire for knowing, we find

---

1   See Isaiah 55:8-9.

that we can more fully know and love the God who made us and loves us.

We are like little children, and God our Father has given us this beautiful scavenger hunt we call science for our delight and our good. Finding the clues and uncovering the next step brings us closer to our Father, brings us joy in the process, and gives us a greater appreciation for the intricacies of the Designer of the hunt. As we search for clues and discover more of the secrets of science, we can join with the psalmist and declare,

> Great are the works of the LORD, studied by all who delight in them. (Ps. 111:2)

> O Lord, how manifold are your works! In wisdom have you made them all; the earth is full of your creatures. (Ps. 104:24)

Appendix: Additional Resources

I would highly recommend reading *Darwin Devolves* by Michael Behe as well as the controversy and discussion surrounding the book. Read both sides! Study the exchange between Behe and some of his most prominent critics/reviewers to see if he's represented fairly and if he can give cogent, scientific arguments/responses:

https://darwindevolves.com/criticism/

I've noted below (using the phrase 'critical exchange') where a back-and-forth dialogue between experts exists for one of these books.

Books promoting materialistic evolution:

Sean Carroll, *The Making of the Fittest: DNA and the Ultimate Forensic Record of Evolution* (W.W. Norton & Company, 2007).

Jerry Coyne, *Why Evolution is True* (Penguin Books, 2010).

Richard Dawkins, *The Blind Watchmaker: Why the Evidence of Evolution Reveals a Universe Without Design* (W.W. Norton & Company, 2015).

Richard Dawkins, *The God Delusion* (Mariner Books, 2008).

Richard Dawkins, *The Greatest Show on Earth: The Evidence for Evolution* (Free Press, 2010).

Daniel Dennett, *Darwin's Dangerous Idea: Evolution and the Meanings of Life* (Simon & Schuster, 1996).

Donald Prothero, *Evolution: What the Fossils Say and Why It Matters* (Columbia University Press, 2017).

Michael Ruse, *Darwin & Design: Does Evolution Have a Purpose?* (Harvard University Press, 2004).

BOOKS ARGUING AGAINST MATERIALISTIC EVOLUTION:

Douglas Axe, *Undeniable: How Biology Confirms Our Intuition That Life Is Designed* (HarperOne, 2016).

Michael Behe, *Darwin Devolves: The New Science About DNA That Challenges Evolution* (HarperOne, 2019).
- Critical Exchange: https://darwindevolves.com/criticism/

Michael Behe, *The Edge of Evolution: The Search for the Limits of Darwinism* (Free Press, 2007).
- Critical Exchange: https://www.discovery.org/a/22661/

John Lennox, *God's Undertaker: Has Science Buried God?* (Lion Hudson, 2009).

John Lennox, *Gunning for God: Why the New Atheists Are Missing the Target* (Lion Hudson, 2011).

Stephen Meyer, *Darwin's Doubt: The Explosive Origin of Animal Life and the Case for Intelligent Design* (HarperOne, 2013).

- Critical Exchange: David Klinghoffer, ed., *Debating Darwin's Doubt: A Scientific Controversy That Can No Longer Be Denied* (Discovery Institute Press, 2015).

Stephen Meyer, *Return of the God Hypothesis: Three Scientific Discoveries That Reveal the Mind Behind the Universe* (HarperOne, 2021).

Stephen Meyer, *Signature in the Cell: DNA and the Evidence for Intelligent Design* (HarperOne, 2009).

- Critical Exchange: David Klinghoffer, ed., *Signature of Controversy: Responses to Critics of Signature in the Cell* (Discovery Institute Press, 2010).

Hugh Ross, *The Creator and the Cosmos: How the Latest Scientific Discoveries Reveal God* 4th Ed. (RTB Press, 2018).

Why Is There Evil in the World (and So Much of It?)

GREG WELTY

Many people argue that the presence of evil in the world is proof that God cannot exist, or if He does exist, cannot be good or all-powerful.

Greg Welty uses biblical exegesis alongside his experience as a philosopher to present a different conclusion. God, the sovereign Creator and Sustainer of the world, really does work all things for good. A must-read for anyone struggling with this issue.

ISBN 978-1-5271-0141-8

How Could a Loving God Send Anyone to Hell?

BENJAMIN M. SKAUG

The question of whether God can be loving and also send people to hell is one people have been asking for a long time. Surely a God who sends people to hell cannot love them? Starting with a look at who God is and how we relate to Him, Benjamin Skaug looks at what the Bible has to say about the difficult topic of hell.

ISBN 978-1-5271-0473-0

Christian Focus Publications

Our mission statement –

STAYING FAITHFUL
In dependence upon God we seek to impact the world
through literature faithful to His infallible Word, the Bible.
Our aim is to ensure that the Lord Jesus Christ is presented
as the only hope to obtain forgiveness of sin, live a useful life
and look forward to heaven with Him.

Our books are published in four imprints:

CHRISTIAN
FOCUS

Popular works including biographies, commentaries, basic
doctrine and Christian living.

CHRISTIAN
HERITAGE

Books representing some of the
best material from the rich heri-
tage of the church.

MENTOR

Books written at a level suitable
for Bible College and seminary
students, pastors, and other serious readers. The imprint includes
commentaries, doctrinal studies,
examination of current issues and
church history.

CF4•K

Children's books for quality Bible
teaching and for all age groups:
Sunday school curriculum, puzzle
and activity books; personal and family devotional titles, biographies and
inspirational stories – because you
are never too young to know Jesus!

Christian Focus Publications Ltd,
Geanies House, Fearn, Ross-shire,
IV20 1TW, Scotland, United Kingdom.
www.christianfocus.com